SECOND EDITION

Workbook

Joan Saslow • Allen Ascher

With Julie C. Rouse

ALWAYS LEARNING

PEARSON

Summit: English for Today's World 1, Second Edition
Workbook

Pearson Education, 10 Bank Street, White Plains, NY 10606

Staff credits: The people who made up the *Summit 1* Workbook team—representing
editorial, production, design, manufacturing, and multimedia—are Rhea Banker, Aerin Csigay,
Dave Dickey, Aliza Greenblatt, Mike Kemper, and Martin Yu.

Text composition: TSI Graphics
Text font: Frutiger 10/12
Cover photograph: Shutterstock.com
Cover design: Elizabeth Carlson

Illustration credits: Steve Attoe: pages 4, 82. Leanne Franson: pages 24, 84. Brian Hughes: page 17. Stephen Hutchings:
page 55 (top). Suzanne Mogensen: page 3. Steve Schulman: page 33. Neil Stewart/NSV: pages 52, 55 (bottom), 92.

Photo credits: p. 6 AP/Wide World Photos; p. 14 ImageSource/age fotostock; p. 15 Schlager Roland/epa/Corbis; p. 22
BananaStock/age fotostock; p. 27 (left) Mary416/Fotolia, (middle) Patrick Robert/ Sygma/Corbis, (right) EPA/UNICEF/Shehzad
Nooran /Landov; p. 31 (left to right) John Springer Collection/Corbis, Muntz/Getty Images, ImageSource/age fotostock, Jacques
Alexandre/age fotostock, Kupka/age fotostock, Angela Wyant/Getty Images, Hulton Archive/Getty Images, SuperStock,
Inc./SuperStock; p. 35 (top) Mauro Fermariello/Photo Researchers, Inc., (bottom) Nicolas Russell/Getty Images; p. 36 Araldo de
Luca/Corbis; p. 44 Photo by Global Volunteers/www.globalvolunteers.org; p. 45 photolibrary/ PictureQuest; p. 53 Park
Street/PhotoEdit, Inc.; p. 61 (1) Monkey Business Images/Dreamstime.com, (2) Hemera/age fotostock, (3) Dave & Les Jacobs/age
fotostock, (4) Plush Studios/age fotostock; p. 62 Fujifotos/The Image Works; p. 72 Bruce Forster/Getty Images; p. 76 ThinkStock
LLC/Photolibrary; p. 78 Digital Vision/age fotostock; p. 84 (1) ImageSource/age fotostock, (2) ImageSource/age fotostock, (3) Con
Tanasiuk/age fotostock, (4) Marcus Mok/Getty Images; p. 85 Keystone/Getty Images; p. 88 Bernardo De Niz/Reuters/Corbis; p. 93
(top left) Sanna Lindberg/age fotostock, (top right) Matthieu Spohn/age fotostock, (bottom left) Digital Vision/age fotostock,
(bottom right) BananaStock/age fotostock.

Text credits: Page 40: "Top Ten Most Annoying Personal Behaviors" reprinted with permission by Donna Dilley, Biz Manners
Columnist, Blue Ridge Business Journal, Roanoke, VA 24011. Page 55: "The Stag with Beautiful Antlers," from *Little Book of Fables*.
Copyright © 2004 by Ediciones Ekaré, Venezuela. English translation copyright © 2004 by Susan Ouriou. First published in English
by Groundwood Books, Ltd. in 2004. Reprinted by permission of the publisher.

ISBN 13: 978-0-13-267987-9
ISBN 10: 0-13-267987-6

Printed in the United States of America

8 9 10–V001–16 15

CONTENTS

New Perspectives

PREVIEW

1 Read the article and take the quiz.

Do You Have What It Takes to Work Abroad?

TRAVEL

Are you bored with your day-to-day life? Sick of the daily grind? If you've had enough of your dull, daily routine, then working in another country may be the life-changing experience you need.

Can you imagine yourself living and working in some far-away location? Maybe you picture yourself working as a computer programmer in Beijing and practicing *tai chi* in your free time. Maybe you'd like to work as an accountant in Sydney and surf on the weekends. What about a job as a nurse in Chicago, a manager in Bangalore, or an engineer in Montreal?

Whatever your dream, now may be the time to go for it. Before you do, take this quiz to see if you have what it takes to work and live abroad.

Circle the statement that describes you best.

1 a. I want adventure in my life.
  b. I like trying new things.
  c. I'm a little uncomfortable in new situations.
  d. I prefer to stay close to home.

2 a. I will eat almost anything.
  b. I like trying different foods.
  c. I prefer foods that are familiar to me.
  d. I won't eat strange food.

3 a. It's fun trying to figure out how to communicate in a new language.
  b. Communicating in a new language is a good experience.
  c. Having to use a new language to communicate is kind of scary.
  d. It's a pain in the neck trying to understand a different language.

4 a. I make new friends easily.
  b. It takes a while for me to make new friends.
  c. It's hard for me to make friends.
  d. I'm shy and do not have many friends.

5 a. I think difficult situations can be good learning experiences.
  b. I work hard to make difficult situations better.
  c. I complain a lot in difficult situations.
  d. If a situation is too difficult, it's probably more trouble than it's worth.

Now figure out your score. Give yourself:

3 points for each **a**.
2 points for each **b**.
1 point for each **c**.
0 points for each **d**.

Score _____

If your score was:

13–15 points	Do it! You'll love working and living overseas.
10–12 points	It may be difficult, but working abroad will be a good experience for you.
7–9 points	You may have to work hard to have a good experience.
0–6 points	Don't do it! You'll be ready to head home after one week.

SOURCE: www.transitionsabroad.com

Do you have what it takes to work and live abroad? Why or why not?

....

....

2 Complete each opinion with an expression from the box. More than one answer is possible for each item.

It's a pain in the neck.	It's more trouble than it's worth.	I can't get enough of it.
I've had about enough of it.	I can't get over how much I enjoy it.	

1. The food here is delicious. _____

2. The weather is terrible here. _____

3. It's too difficult to get there, and there isn't a lot to see. _____

4. I have to work hard to understand what people are saying. _____

5. Being here is so much fun. _____

LESSON 1

3 Complete each sentence with the gerund or infinitive form of the verb in parentheses.

a. Don't forget (call) _____ your mother on her birthday.

b. Stop (eat) _____ sweets and fatty foods.

c. Remember (make) _____ time for just the two of you.

d. I'll never forget (meet) _____ my boss for the first time.

e. Every now and then, you should stop (tell) _____ the people you know how much they mean to you.

Now match each sentence above with a topic below. Write the letter on the line.

1. _____ health   3. _____ family   5. _____ romance

2. _____ friends   4. _____ work

4 Challenge. Answer the questions about yourself.

1. What will you never forget about your childhood?

    Example: *I'll never forget baking holiday cookies with my grandmother.*

    _____

    _____

2. When you're eighty years old, what do you think you'll remember about your life now?

    Example: *I'll remember going to the beach with my friends.*

    _____

    _____

5 Write a tip or reminder for each person. Use <u>remember</u>, <u>forget</u>, or <u>stop</u> with a gerund or an infinitive. Use the phrases in parentheses.

1. ....
(buy coffee)

2. ....
(wish your wife happy anniversary)

3. ....
(work so much)

4. ....
(turn off your cell phone)

LESSON 2

6 Complete the conversation. Write the letter on the line.

A: Have you met our new neighbors, the Lovinas?

B: ....
    1.

A: Well, the husband is friendly. He seems like a nice guy.

B: ....
    2.

A: She's never home. Everyone says she's a workaholic.

B: ....
    3.

A: She works in advertising, I think. She's a manager.

B: ....
    4.

A: Well, the least we can do is keep an open mind. She might turn out to be really likeable.

a. And the wife? I wonder what she's like.

b. So, she's a boss . . . I hope she's not anything like *my* boss!

c. No, I haven't had a chance yet. What are they like?

d. Really? What does she do?

In Japan, 76 percent of people work more than 40 hours per week. In Germany, 44 percent of people work more than 40 hours per week.

SOURCE: www.nationmaster.com

New Perspectives **3**

7 Read the descriptions of Type A and Type B personalities. Then answer the questions.

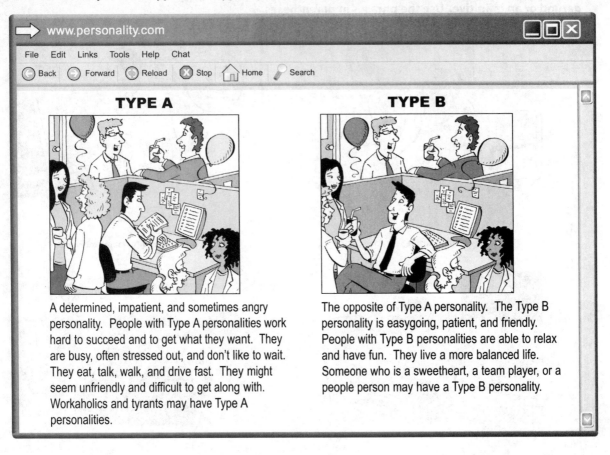

www.personality.com

File   Edit   Links   Tools   Help   Chat

Back   Forward   Reload   Stop   Home   Search

TYPE A

A determined, impatient, and sometimes angry personality. People with Type A personalities work hard to succeed and to get what they want. They are busy, often stressed out, and don't like to wait. They eat, talk, walk, and drive fast. They might seem unfriendly and difficult to get along with. Workaholics and tyrants may have Type A personalities.

TYPE B

The opposite of Type A personality. The Type B personality is easygoing, patient, and friendly. People with Type B personalities are able to relax and have fun. They live a more balanced life. Someone who is a sweetheart, a team player, or a people person may have a Type B personality.

1. Do you know someone who has a Type A personality? ....

2. What is this person like? Write three examples to support your opinion.

....

....

....

3. Describe your own personality. Are you more like a Type A or a Type B personality?

....

....

....

8 What qualities would you like the people in your life to have? Complete the sentences with adjectives from the box.

easygoing	fun	helpful	polite	reliable	smart
fair	funny	lovable	outgoing	serious	talkative
friendly	hardworking	modest	professional	silly	

1. I would like a boss who's ....

2. I would like co-workers who are ....

3. I would like a spouse who's ....

4. I would like classmates who are ....

   5. I would like friends who are ....

   6. I would like neighbors who are ....

   7. I would like a teacher who's ....

   8. I would like to be more ....

9 **Complete the conversation with your own words.**

   A: Have you had a chance to meet .... ?

   B: No, I haven't. I wonder what .... like.

   A: Well, everyone says ....

   B: Yeah, but you can't believe everything you hear. ....

LESSON 3

10 **Read each adjective. Does it describe an optimistic or a pessimistic perspective? Write O for optimistic or P for pessimistic.**

   1. .... down

   2. .... defeated

   3. .... hopeful

   4. .... positive

   5. .... negative

   6. .... cynical

   Now read each statement. Write O for optimistic or P for pessimistic.

   1. .... The glass is half full.

   2. .... The glass is half empty.

   3. .... Times are hard now, but life will get better.

   4. .... Life will always be difficult and painful.

   5. .... The world is unjust and unfair.

   6. .... There's beauty, love, generosity, and goodness in the world.

11 **Complete each suggestion with the gerund or infinitive form of the verb in parentheses.**

   1. Remember (look) .... on the bright side.

   2. Stop (expect) .... the worst.

   3. Don't forget (see) .... goodness in the world.

   4. Stop (believe) .... that life will always be difficult and painful.

   5. Remember (avoid) .... negative thinking.

   6. Don't forget (try) .... to see a solution.

12 Reading Warm-up. **Answer the questions.**

1. Do you know someone who is very optimistic? Who? ....

2. Do you know who Lance Armstrong is? What do you know about him?

....

....

13 Reading. **Read the article about Lance Armstrong. Then answer the questions.**

VOL. 55 | **The Power of Optimism**

Martin Seligman has been studying optimists and pessimists for 25 years. He's a psychologist and the author of bestselling books that help people to be more optimistic. In his studies of world-class athletes and top performers in the business world, Seligman found that optimists perform better when they encounter difficult situations than pessimists do. According to Seligman, "When pessimists come up against an obstacle, they often quit; when optimists meet an obstacle, they try harder." An optimist stays in the game and instead of seeing a problem, looks for a solution.

One world-class athlete who stayed in the game and is a perfect example of the power of optimism is the cyclist Lance Armstrong. In 1996, Armstrong was diagnosed with advanced testicular cancer that had spread to his lungs and brain. His doctors were not optimistic, but he was. Instead of feeling down and defeated by his serious condition, Armstrong felt challenged and prepared for his future. He found chemotherapy treatments that would not damage his lungs permanently (because a world-class cyclist needs strong lungs). He rode his bicycle 80 to 100 kilometers a day, even though he was so sick that it was difficult for him to get out of bed. And, he had his sperm frozen so that he could have children someday, even though he was single at the time.

Armstrong survived cancer and won the Tour de France seven times. He has three children, a boy and twin girls.   Lance Armstrong has been called a "hope machine" and is an inspiration for those of us who need help being optimistic.

SOURCES: www.coachginger.com
Learned Optimism: How to Change Your Mind and Your Life, Martin Seligman (New York, Pocket Books, 1998)

---

1. What was Lance Armstrong's difficult situation? ....

2. How did he respond to this problem? ....

....

3. Did he succeed? ....

4. Were his hopes realistic? Explain your answer. ....

....

14 **Think of a problem you have or a difficult situation you're facing. What's the problem or situation?**

....

....

Now try to "see a solution." What are three things you could do to make the situation better?

1. ....

2. ....

3. ....

15 Match the perspectives with their definitions.

1. .... optimistic
2. .... pessimistic
3. .... realistic

a. expecting that bad things will happen in the future or that a situation will have a bad result

b. believing that good things will happen in the future, or feeling confident that you will succeed

c. perceiving and responding to situations in a practical way, according to what is actually possible

What's your perspective? Explain your answer. ....
....

Challenge. **How does the realist see the glass of water?**
....

> "Keep a green tree in your heart and perhaps the singing bird will come."
> — Chinese proverb

LESSON 4

16 **What About You?** **Answer the questions about your own experiences.**

1. Describe an experience that <u>broadened your horizons</u> — or made it possible for you to learn, understand, and do new things. ....
....

2. Describe a <u>rewarding</u> experience you've had — an experience that made you feel happy and satisfied because you were doing something useful, important, or interesting, even if you did not earn much money. ....
....

3. Describe an experience that caused you to <u>see the big picture</u> — or made you realize what was really important in your life. ....
....

17 **After completing Student's Book page 11 in class, write what you remember about a classmate's life-changing experience.**

Grammar Booster

A Circle the gerund or infinitive form of the verb to correctly complete each sentence.

1. Mr. Banks often urges his wife **coming** / **to come** home from work earlier.

2. He wants her **spending** / **to spend** more time with her family.

3. She promises **trying** / **to try**, but she's really not capable of **slowing** / **to slow** down.

4. She's sorry **disappointing** / **to disappoint** her family, but she's also worried about **advancing** / **to advance** in her career.

5. Mrs. Banks knows it's important **living** / **to live** a balanced life, but she keeps **working** / **to work** late and **bringing** / **to bring** work home on the weekends.

6. She plans **taking** / **to take** some time off next month, but don't be surprised if demands at work prevent her from **doing** / **to do** so.

B Complete each sentence with your own gerund or infinitive phrase. Refer to Student's Book pages A3 and A4 if you need to.

1. I look forward to ....

2. I miss ....

3. I'm fortunate ....

4. I struggle ....

5. I can't stand ....

6. My parents encouraged me ....

7. .... is relaxing for me.

8. It's my dream ....

9. I'm tired of ....

10. I'm studying English ....

C List three ideas under each of the topics below.

1. **Activities you enjoy**

....

....

....

2. **Your goals**

....

....

....

3. **Good memories**

....

....

....

4. **To-do list for this week**

....

....

....

Now use your lists to complete the sentences. Use gerunds or infinitives. Make sure the items in each series are parallel.

Example: I enjoy *skiing, running, and painting* ....

1. I enjoy ....

2. I intend ....

3. I recall ....

4. I need ....

Writing: Describe optimists or pessimists

A Prewriting. Brainstorming ideas. Write words and phrases related to each perspective.

Optimists

think positively ....

....

....

....

Pessimists

think negatively ....

....

....

....

Use your ideas to write a topic sentence for each perspective. (Remember: The topic sentence **introduces** the topic and the focus of the paragraph.)

1. Optimists: ....

2. Pessimists: ....

Choose one of your topic sentences. Write three to five supporting sentences. (Remember: The supporting sentences give **details**, **examples**, and **other facts** related to the topic sentence.)

1. ....

2. ....

3. ....

4. ....

5. ....

B Writing. Write your topic sentence and supporting sentences from Exercise A in the form of a paragraph. End with a concluding sentence. (Remember: The concluding sentence **restates** [gives the same information in different words] the topic sentence or **summarizes** the paragraph.)

....

....

....

....

....

....

....

C Self-Check.

☐ Does your paragraph have a topic sentence?

☐ Do the supporting sentences in your paragraph all relate to the topic?

☐ Do you have a concluding sentence?

UNIT 2

Musical Moods

PREVIEW

1 Try to name an artist for each musical genre.

1. Pop: ....

2. Rock: ....

3. Urban dance: ....

4. World: ....

5. Latin: ....

6. Jazz: ....

7. Classical: ....

2 Complete the chart.

What types of music do you listen to when you're . . .
1. studying?
2. eating in a restaurant?
3. dancing?
4. feeling down?
5. commuting (by car, bus, train, etc.)?

3 Complete the conversation about musical tastes. Use your own words.

A: So, what's in your CD collection?

B: ....

A: Let's put something on.

B: How about .... ?

A: What's it like?

B: ....

4 **What About You?** **Answer the questions.**

1. What was the last CD you bought? ....

2. Circle the adjectives you'd use to describe the CD.

annoying	different	exciting	offensive	surprising	uplifiting
brilliant	dull	fun	playful	traditional	
cynical	energetic	haunting	romantic	unpredictable	

3. Which songs on the CD do you like the most? The least? ....

....

5 **Read the online music review.**

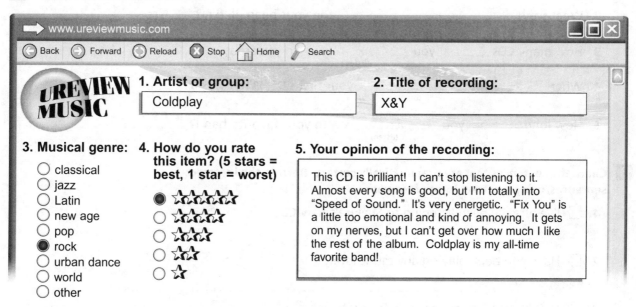

Now complete a review of the CD you chose in Exercise 4.

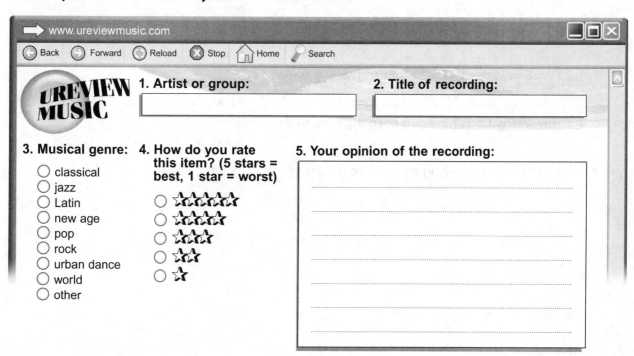

LESSON 1

6 For each description, name a song, a band, or a singer you know.

1. A song with a great dance beat: ....

2. A band with a unique sound: ....

3. A song with a catchy melody: ....

4. A singer with an amazing voice: ....

5. A song with fantastic lyrics: ....

7 Complete the questions with the simple past tense or the present perfect continuous form of the verb in parentheses. Then answer the questions.

1. What .... you .... to lately? ....
   (listen)

2. What song .... you .... in your head all day? ....
   (hum)

3. How many CDs .... you .... to yesterday? ....
   (listen)

4. When .... you .... your first CD? What was it? ....
   (buy)

5. How long .... you .... to your favorite band? ....
   (listen)

8 Check the sentences that are grammatically correct. Rewrite the incorrect sentences, using a correct form of the verb.

1. ☐ I've already been listening to Shakira's new CD.

   ....

2. ☐ Have you been playing any music lately?

   ....

3. ☐ He's been going to concerts for a while.

   ....

4. ☐ She's been going to five concerts this month.

   ....

5. ☐ I've seen Vanessa-Mae in concert twice.

   ....

6. ☐ How many times have you been listening to that song?

   ....

7. ☐ Have you been playing my favorite song yet?

   ....

LESSON 2

9 **Check the statements that you agree with.**

1. ☐ I can't imagine what my life would be like without music.
2. ☐ Listening to music is how I stay productive.
3. ☐ Music is what helps me unwind.
4. ☐ Music is a way for people to communicate with whomever they meet.
5. ☐ Music is a way for me to express what's in my heart.

10 **Complete each noun clause with your own words.**

1. I wonder who ....

2. I don't understand why ....

3. I'm not sure when ....

4. I don't know where ....

5. I have no idea what ....

6. Can you tell me which .... ?

7. I can't imagine how ....

11 **Read each situation. Then use noun clauses to complete the sentences in your own words.**

1. Your friend invites you to a concert. You need more information. You ask him _when the_
   concert is and who's playing ....

2. You need to buy a gift for your nephew. You ask his mother ....
   ....

3. You're discussing music with some friends. You say that to you, listening to music is ....
   ....

4. Your colleague has just met a famous musician. You want to know ....
   ....

12 Read about the role of music in Adam Reed's life. Underline the eight noun clauses.

I'm not sure when I started really listening to music. I think I was about 14. I was totally into pop music then. Now pop music gets on my nerves. I listen to urban dance music mostly, and jazz or classical when I'm working or studying. My taste in music has changed over the years, but the role of music in my life has not changed. I've been listening for almost ten years now, and I can't imagine what I would do without music. Listening to music is how I spend my free time, and it's what helps me focus and get things done. It's how I relax and how I have fun with my friends. I believe that life would be dull and empty without music.

Adam Reed
San Francisco, California, USA

Now write a short paragraph about the role of music in your life. Why do you listen to music? What types of music do you listen to? How has your taste changed? Try to use noun clauses.

LESSON 3

13 Do you know someone who's gifted? What does this person do well? Describe his/her personality. What are some of this person's positive qualities? Negative qualities?

....

....

....

14 **Reading.** Answer the question. Then read the biography on page 15.

Have you ever heard of Ray Charles? What do you know about him?

....

....

14 UNIT 2

Ray Charles

"I was born with music inside me."

They called him "The Genius"—"the *only* genius in the [music] business," according to singer Frank Sinatra. What made him a genius is the original way in which he combined the diverse genres of jazz, rhythm and blues, gospel, and country. He broke down the walls that had always existed between musical genres, creating groundbreaking music that has had a huge influence on the course of rock and pop. It has been said that his music can "break your heart or make you dance." His name was Ray Charles, and he was known as "the father of soul."

Ray Charles was born in 1930, into a poor family in the southeastern United States. At age five, he gradually began to lose his vision and was totally blind by age seven.

Charles had shown an interest in music since the age of three. At seven, he left home to attend the Florida School for the Deaf and Blind. There he learned to read, write, and arrange music in Braille and play the piano, organ, saxophone, clarinet, and trumpet. While he was at the school, his mother died. At fifteen, he left school and began working as a traveling jazz musician in Florida, and later in Washington state.

In 1950, Charles moved to Los Angeles, where he found his own unique sound. He combined jazz and blues with gospel music to create his first big hit recording, "I Got a Woman." On "I Got a Woman," Charles began to sing in a more emotional, intense, and exciting voice. He later said, "When I started to sing like myself . . . when I started singing like Ray Charles, it had this spiritual and churchy, this religious or gospel sound." This recording made him famous and marked the beginning of a new musical genre, "soul."

Although Charles had discovered his sound and success, he didn't stop trying new things.

Always energetic, he explored new genres and brought his unique style to new audiences. In the 1960s, he had both country and pop hits, with songs like "Georgia on My Mind" and "Hit the Road, Jack."

Throughout his life, Charles continued to write and perform. He also made television and movie appearances. His participation in the 1985 release of "We Are the World" brought a renewed interest in his work.

To this day, Ray Charles remains one of the most important influences on popular music. His passionate singing and intelligent combining of different musical genres is the ideal that many musicians continue to measure their work by.

Ray Charles died on June 10, 2004, at the age of 73. A notorious ladies' man, he is survived by 12 children, 18 grandchildren, and 1 great-grandchild. In response to the news of his death, singer Aretha Franklin said, "He was a fabulous man, full of humor and wit . . ." Ray Charles possessed all of the positive qualities of a creative personality—he was gifted, energetic, imaginative, and passionate—without displaying the negative qualities that often accompany creative genius. He was not difficult or egotistical. In fact, he was quite humble. In 1983 he said, "Music's been around a long time, and there's going to be music long after Ray Charles is dead. I just want to make my mark, leave something musically good behind."

Sources: www.pbs.org, www.en.wikipedia.org, www.swingmusic.net

List at least six adjectives from the reading that describe Ray Charles's music.

....

....

....

Now list five adjectives from the reading that describe Ray Charles's personality.

....

....

....

15 **Match the words and phrases from the reading with their definitions.**

1. .... groundbreaking
2. .... blind
3. .... Braille
4. .... gospel
5. .... soul
6. .... ladies' man
7. .... humble

a. a type of music with jazz, blues, and gospel influences that often expresses deep emotions

b. a form of raised printing that blind people can read by touching

c. original and important; showing a new way of doing or thinking about things

d. not considering yourself better than others

e. not able to see

f. a man who enjoys and attracts the company of women

g. a style of religious music associated with the southern U.S.

16 **Write a short description of Ray Charles's music, based on the reading.**

....

....

....

17 **Challenge. What do Ludwig van Beethoven and Ray Charles have in common? How are they different? Fill in the diagram to compare them.**

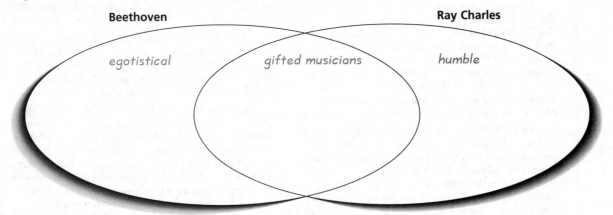

Beethoven   Ray Charles

egotistical   gifted musicians   humble

LESSON 4

18 **Complete the sentences with the correct participial adjectives. Use the present or past participle of the underlined verb.**

1. Classical music <u>soothes</u> her infant son.

   a. Classical music is .... to her infant son.

   b. Her infant son is .... by classical music.

2. Jazz <u>interests</u> Robert.

   a. Robert thinks jazz is ....

   b. Robert is .... in jazz.

3. Her piano playing <u>amazes</u> me.

   a. I'm .... by her piano playing.

   b. Her piano playing is ....

4. The song's lyrics <u>touched</u> Samantha.

   a. Samantha was .... by the song's lyrics.

   b. Samantha found the song's lyrics to be very ....

5. Pop music <u>bores</u> Eric because it's so predictable.

    a. Eric is .... by predictable pop music.

    b. Eric thinks pop music is .... and predictable.

6. Concerts <u>excite</u> Alex and Sophie. They're going to one this Saturday.

    a. Alex and Sophie think concerts are ....

    b. Alex and Sophie are .... about the concert on Saturday.

19 **Circle the correct adjective and then complete each sentence with your own words.**

1. I'm (soothed / soothing) by ....

2. I find .... to be very (entertained / entertaining).

3. I try to avoid .... because it's so (depressed / depressing).

4. I was (disappointed / disappointing) when I found out that ....

5. For me, ... is really (relaxed / relaxing).

6. I'm (pleased / pleasing) that ....

20 **Read the advertisement. Then answer the questions.**

1. According to the ad, what are five benefits of *Little Genius* CDs?

....

....

....

....

2. What's your opinion? Do you think listening to music is beneficial for babies?

....

....

Grammar Booster

A Choose the correct verb form(s) to complete each sentence. In some sentences, two or more verb forms are correct.

1. He .... to pop music when he was a teenager.

   ☐ listened   ☐ has listened   ☐ has been listening

2. They .... new-age music all day, and it's starting to get on my nerves.

   ☐ played   ☐ have played   ☐ have been playing

3. By the time I got to the concert, my favorite singer ....

   ☐ already performed   ☐ had already performed   ☐ had already been performing

4. He .... that music video last night on TV.

   ☐ saw   ☐ has seen   ☐ has been seeing

5. She .... on the lyrics for her new song for hours, but now she's taking a break for dinner.

   ☐ worked   ☐ has worked   ☐ has been working

B Find the error in each sentence. Rewrite the sentence, using a correct verb form.

1. What did you listen to lately?

   ....

2. Sarah Cho has been playing that CD for me yesterday.

   ....

3. I've been watching that video four times already.

   ....

4. I was buying that DVD yesterday.

   ....

5. How many concerts have you been going to?

   ....

6. The performance already began by the time we arrived.

   ....

7. When we got to the ticket window, the concert already sold out.

   ....

8. Many people have been downloading world music last year.

   ....

C Complete the sentences with your own words. Use appropriate verb forms.

1. When I began this class, I had already _____.

2. Before I traveled to _____, I had never _____.

3. I had never seen _____ until _____.

4. I bought the _____ CD after _____.

5. By the time I got home last night, _____.

D Read each pair of sentences. Then write one sentence with a similar meaning, using the past perfect continuous.

1. He worked at Datatech for 35 years. Then he retired.

   He had been working at Datatech for 35 years when he retired.

2. She slept for only four hours. Then her alarm clock went off.

   _____

3. They drove their car for ten years. Then it broke down.

   _____

4. I waited for 45 minutes. Then the train arrived.

   _____

5. We lived in London for five years. Then we decided to move to Dublin.

   _____

E Complete each statement in your own way.

Example: Many people believe that *there is life on other planets*.

1. Many people believe that _____.

2. My friend argues that _____.

3. Experts recommend that _____.

4. Some people claim that _____.

5. The newspapers report that _____.

Now give your opinion of each statement, using a noun clause as a noun complement.

Example: [The belief . . .] *The belief that there is life on other planets makes sense to me.*

1. [The belief . . .] _____.

2. [The argument . . .] _____.

3. [The recommendation . . .] _____.

4. [The claim . . .] _____.

5. [The report . . .] _____.

Writing: Describe a friend or a relative

A **Prewriting. Clustering ideas.** Create an idea cluster about a friend or relative you know well.

   a. Write the person's name inside the center circle below.

   b. Use the idea cluster to describe the person. Write ideas that come to mind in the circles around the main circle. You can include personality traits, interests, accomplishments, personal qualities, occupation, etc.

   c. Use the circles connected to each of those circles to expand or give details about your ideas. Try to write something in each circle, but it's OK if some circles are empty.

B **Writing.** Write a paragraph describing your friend or relative, using the information from your cluster. Make sure to use parallel structure.

....

....

....

....

....

....

....

....

C **Self-Check.**

   ☐ Did you use parallel structure with pairs or series of nouns, adjectives, and adverbs?

   ☐ Did you use parallel structure with the clauses, phrases, and tenses?

   ☐ Does the topic sentence introduce the topic of the paragraph?

Money Matters

PREVIEW

1 How can you spend less and save more? List some ideas.

1. ....

2. ....

3. ....

4. ....

5. ....

> 1. Bring lunch to work instead of buying it.
> 2. Take the bus to work instead of driving.
> 3. Remember to pay credit card bills on time. Avoid late charges!

2 Read each statement. Check the statements that are good financial advice.

1. ☐ Keep track of your expenses.

2. ☐ If you don't have enough money for something, use your credit card to treat yourself.

3. ☐ Buy financial planning software.

4. ☐ Cut back on your spending.

5. ☐ Live beyond your means.

6. ☐ Wait until you're older to start saving.

7. ☐ Make sure your income is more than your expenses.

8. ☐ Pay the least possible amount on your credit card bills each month.

9. ☐ Put some money away in savings each month.

10. ☐ If you're feeling down, go shopping.

3 Answer the questions.

1. What's a minor indulgence (something small and unnecessary) that you spend money on regularly? (For example, a daily cup of coffee or a weekly magazine.) ....

2. How much does this indulgence cost? ....

3. Calculate how many times per year you spend money on it. (For example, a cup of coffee each weekday: 5 days x 52 weeks = 260 times per year.) ....

4. Multiply the cost (your answer to question 2) by the number of times (your answer to question 3). How much money do you spend in a year on your small indulgence? ....

5. Were you surprised by the results? Can you think of something else you'd like to spend that money on? ....

4 **Read the article.**

Financial Planning
Five Benefits of Keeping a Budget

1. A budget allows you to spend money on things you really need or want. A budget requires you to keep track of your expenses. You see where your money actually goes and plan where to cut back on spending. The money you used to spend daily on little things like coffee or taxis can go toward something more important.

2. A budget can keep you out of debt. With a budget, you know whether or not you're living within your means. If you use credit cards, this may not be obvious. You might have extra cash at the end of each month and think that you're OK. But, if you're not paying your credit card bills in full, you're probably living beyond your means.

3. A budget can make you better prepared for emergencies. A budget requires you to put some money away in savings. So, if you find yourself in a difficult situation or faced with unexpected expenses, you'll have some extra money you can fall back on.

4. A budget can help you reach your savings goals. Whatever you are saving for, you need a plan that tells you how much you have, how much you need to spend, and how much you can save.

5. A budget gives you peace of mind because it allows you to stop worrying about how you're going to make ends meet.

SOURCE: www.financialplan.about.com

Now answer the questions.

1. According to the article, why is it important to keep track of your expenses?

   ....

2. According to the article, why can using credit cards be a problem?

   ....

3. Why can a budget make you better prepared for emergencies?

   ....

4. Which benefit from the article do you think is the most important? Why?

   ....

5 **Respond to the e-mail. Write three suggestions for how the person could budget his money to save for a TV.**

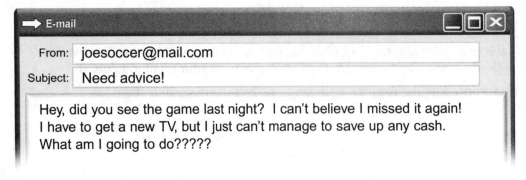

E-mail

From: joesoccer@mail.com

Subject: Need advice!

Hey, did you see the game last night? I can't believe I missed it again!
I have to get a new TV, but I just can't manage to save up any cash.
What am I going to do?????

....

....

....

....

LESSON 1

6 Answer each question about your financial goals. Then, for each answer, do the following:

    a. Write a sentence about what you will do to reach your goal. Use <u>expect</u>, <u>hope</u>, <u>intend</u>, or <u>plan</u> with an infinitive.

    b. Write a sentence about when your goal will be reached. Use the future perfect.

Example: What's something expensive that you hope to buy? *a laptop computer*

    a. *I intend to put away $100 in savings each month.*

    b. *I will have saved enough to buy a laptop by next March.*

1. What's something expensive that you hope to buy?

    a.

    b.

2. Do you have a debt you'd like to pay off? What is it?

    a.

    b.

3. What is one way you can cut back on your spending and save more each month?

    a.

    b.

7 What will you have done by the year 2020? Write a short paragraph. Use the future perfect or <u>expect</u>, <u>hope</u>, <u>intend</u>, or <u>plan</u> and the perfect form of an infinitive.

Example: *By the year 2020, I will have finished law school. I expect to have bought a house by then. I hope to have gotten married and started a family...*

LESSON 2

8 Look at the pictures. Why do the people regret their purchases? Complete each explanation with a reason from the box.

is so hard to operate	takes up so much room	is so hard to put together
just sits around collecting dust	costs so much to maintain	

1. "I bought a guitar last summer. I really intended to learn how to play it, but I haven't picked it up for months now. It ...."

2. "I was so excited to get my new PDA. But it .... Who has thumbs small enough to push those tiny buttons? Not me! What a pain!"

3. "We bought a beautiful crib for our baby, but it's in pieces all over the floor. Unfortunately, the instructions are in Italian, and it ...."

4. "I ordered a new computer online, but I had no idea the monitor would be so big. It .... on my desk. I should have bought a laptop."

5. "I wish I hadn't bought this boat. I don't use it very often, and it .... Between the fuel, the docking fees, and the costs to service and clean it, I'm not sure it's worth it."

9 For each item in Exercise 8, write a sentence about the buyer's remorse.
Use the inverted form of the past unreal conditional.

1. *Had he known it would just sit around collecting dust, he wouldn't have bought a guitar.*

2. _____

3. _____

4. _____

5. _____

10 After completing the Now You Can on Student's Book page 31, write a statement
expressing buyer's remorse about the purchase listed there or about another
purchase. Use the inverted form of the past unreal conditional.

LESSON 3

11 Read the following excerpts from the radio call-in show on Student's Book page 32.
Try to determine the meaning of the underlined phrases from their context.

Steve:	"I'm afraid I'm really having problems <u>making ends meet</u> . . . I earn a good living, but it seems like no matter how much money I make, I can't seem to catch up."
Lara:	"Do you <u>put anything away for a rainy day?</u>"
Steve:	"You mean savings? No way. There's never enough for that."
Lara:	"Steve, what about debt? Are you <u>maxing out</u> on your credit cards?"
Steve:	"Well, yes, I do use credit cards, if that's what you mean."
Lara:	"Are you drowning in credit card bills, or have they been fairly reasonable so far?"
Steve:	"Well . . . I guess I'd have to say I've been <u>drowning in debt</u>."
Lara:	"Steve, if you want to <u>keep your head above water</u>, you've got to <u>live within your means</u>. That means spending less than you're making, not more."
Lara:	"If you feel like your finances are out of control, then you need to <u>take the bull by the horns</u> and take control of your finances."

Now match the phrases on the left with the definitions on the right. Write the letter on the line.

1. _____ make ends meet

2. _____ put something away for a rainy day

3. _____ max out

4. _____ drown in debt

5. _____ keep your head above water

6. _____ live within your means

7. _____ take the bull by the horns

a. owe so much money that your financial situation is almost impossible to deal with

b. have just enough money to buy what you need

c. use something to its limit or so much that there is nothing left

d. manage to deal with all your debts or some other problem, but it's so difficult that you almost can't do it

e. to save something, especially money, for a time when you will need it

f. to take control of a difficult situation

g. to spend only the money or income that you have, no more

12 Circle the letter of the correct choice to complete each statement.

1. Spendthrifts generally live .... their means.

   a. below   **b.** within   **c.** beyond

2. Big spenders are more likely to ....

   a. be drowning in debt   **b.** be frugal   **c.** stick to a budget

3. Cheapskates generally ....

   a. use credit cards often   **b.** have a lot of stuff   **c.** keep track of their expenses

4. Big spenders are usually ....

   a. generous   **b.** stingy   **c.** frugal

5. Thrifty people are more likely to ....

   a. be wiped out by a job loss   **b.** stick to a budget   **c.** let their bills get out of hand

13 Do you know someone who's a big spender, a spendthrift, or a tightwad? Describe his/her spending habits. Give examples.

> The world record for owning the most credit cards is held by Walter Cavanagh of Santa Clara, California, USA. He has 1,397 cards, which together are worth more than $1.65 million in credit.

SOURCE: www.guinnessworldrecords.com

LESSON 4

14 Reading Warm-up. Complete the chart with information about a charity with which you are familiar.

Name of charity	Who they help	What they do
CARE	poor people all over the world	work to reduce poverty and solve problems in poor communities—through education, health care, etc.

Have you ever donated money to a charity? What was the name of the organization or cause? Why did you make a donation?

....

....

....

World Wildlife Fund

The World Wildlife Fund (WWF) is known worldwide by its panda logo. WWF has been working for almost 50 years in more than 100 countries around the globe to conserve nature and the diversity of life on Earth. With more than 5 million members worldwide, WWF is the world's largest privately-financed conservation organization. It leads international efforts to protect animals, plants, and natural areas. Its global goals are:

1. to save endangered species—especially giant pandas, tigers, threatened whales and dolphins, rhinos, elephants, marine turtles, and great apes.
2. to protect the habitats where these endangered species and other wild animals live.
3. to address threats to the natural environment—such as pollution, over-fishing, and climate change.

Doctors Without Borders

Doctors Without Borders (Médecins Sans Frontières, or MSF) is an international independent humanitarian organization that provides emergency medical assistance in almost 70 countries. Each year, MSF medical and non-medical volunteers participate in more than 3,400 aid missions. These international volunteers work with more than 16,000 people hired locally to provide medical care. They often work in the most remote or dangerous parts of the world to do things such as provide health care, get hospitals up and running, perform surgery, vaccinate children, operate feeding centers, and offer psychological care. MSF gets medical attention to people who need it in cases of:

1. war or armed conflict.
2. epidemics of infectious diseases such as tuberculosis, malaria, and AIDS.
3. natural disasters.
4. non-existent health care in remote areas.

The United Nations Children's Fund

The United Nations Children's Fund (UNICEF) is active in 157 countries and territories around the world. The organization works to improve the lives of children worldwide. Its mission is to ensure every child's right to health, education, equality, and protection. UNICEF's priorities are:

1. ensuring quality basic education for all children, especially girls.
2. reaching every child with vaccines and other life-saving health services.
3. building protective environments to keep children safe from violence, abuse, and exploitation.
4. preventing the spread of HIV/AIDS among young people and from parent to child and providing care for those already affected.
5. giving each and every child the best start in life—through health services, good nutrition, safe water, and early learning activities.

SOURCES: www.worldwildlife.org, www.doctorswithoutborders.org, www.unicef.org

Now complete the chart with information from the reading.

Name of charity	Who they help	What they do

16 To which of the three charities on page 27 would you consider making a contribution? Is there one you wouldn't want to give money to? What are your reasons for donating or not donating?

....

....

....

> " Charity begins at home
> but should not end there. "
> —Scottish proverb

SOURCE: www.charityvillage.com

Grammar Booster

A What are your plans? For each item, write a sentence about what you will probably be doing. Use the future continuous.

1. Next Monday I ....

2. This weekend I ....

3. Next year I ....

4. Five years from now I ....

5. At this time next week I ....

B Imagine your life in ten years. Where will you be living? What are you going to be doing? Write a paragraph, using the future continuous. When the future continuous is not possible, use the simple future tense.

C Look at the two schedules. Write sentences comparing the activities of Tom and Tina Lee for each day. Use a time clause with <u>while</u> and the future continuous.

Tom Lee

Thursday	work
Friday	work
Saturday	clean the house
Sunday	do laundry

Tina Lee

Thursday	pack for weekend trip with friends
Friday	lie on the beach
Saturday	go horseback riding
Sunday	play tennis

1. Thursday: *While Tom Lee is working, Tina Lee is going to be packing for a trip.*

2. Friday: _____

3. Saturday: _____

4. Sunday: _____

D Complete the chart with three of your hobbies or activities and the year in which you started each.

Hobby / activity	When started

Now use the information in the chart to complete the sentences, using the future perfect continuous.

Example: By the year 2013, *I will have been collecting stamps for 20 years* .

1. By the year 2015, _____ .

2. By next year, _____ .

3. By the time I _____, I _____ .

Writing: Describe a new charitable organization

A **Prewriting. Listing ideas.** Choose an idea for a new local charity. Think of a name and long-term goal for your charity. Then complete the chart.

Name: ....

Long-term goal: ....

Some ideas
• An organization to improve city parks
• An after-school program for young children
• A fund to provide housing for the homeless
• An organization to help stray animals
• A soup kitchen
• Your own idea: ....

WRITING MODEL

The mission of People for City Park is to make the park a clean, safe, and fun place for families to spend time outdoors. First, we plan to clean up the park. We will post signs in the community and ask for volunteers. Next, we intend to ask local nurseries to donate new trees, plants, and flowers for the park. Then, we hope to raise money for new playground equipment. We will place collection jars in cafes, restaurants, and shops. In the end, we expect to have collected enough money and bought new equipment for children to play on by next summer.

	Goal or step	Plan	Completion date
First,			
Next,			
Then,			
In the end,			

B **Writing.** Write a paragraph, using ideas from your chart. Your topic sentence should state your charity's long-term goal. Use time order words and expressions to organize the sequence of steps in your paragraph.

....

....

....

....

....

....

....

C **Self-Check.**

☐ Did you use time order words or expressions in the paragraph?

☐ Does the sequence of events in the paragraph make sense?

☐ Does the topic sentence introduce the topic of the paragraph?

Looking Good

PREVIEW

1 Look at the hairstyles. Then answer the questions.

a bouffant

a mullet

an afro

a Mohawk

a bob

a Caesar cut

a quiff

a shag cut

1. Do you find any of these hairstyles attractive? Which ones?

2. Do you find any of these hairstyles unattractive? Which ones?

3. Do any of the hairstyles look modern, like you might see them in a fashion magazine today?

4. Which hairstyles are attention-getting?

5. Which hairstyles look like they take a lot of time to maintain?

6. Would you consider any of these hairstyles for yourself? Which one(s)?

2 Complete the sentences about your favorite outfit.

1. I love to wear my   .

2. These clothes are formal / casual. (Circle one.)

3. If I wore this outfit to   , I would be underdressed.

4. If I wore this outfit to   , I would be overdressed.

5. If I wore this outfit to   , I would be appropriately dressed.

LESSON 1

3 Read the opinions of casual business dress. Check the statements with which you agree.

1. ☐ What's important is to act like a professional. If you're confident and good at your job, you can be just as effective in jeans and a nice shirt as in a suit and tie.

2. ☐ I think casual dress is appropriate for most offices, as long as one's appearance is clean and neat.

3. ☐ I believe that when people dress like professionals, they act more professionally.

4. ☐ I think dress-down day is a pain in the neck. I never know what to wear. What does "business casual" really mean?

5. ☐ People have taken casual dress codes too far! A number of companies have actually had to introduce "business formal days."

6. ☐ I don't think casual dress creates a good image for a company, especially if the company does business internationally.

7. ☐ Casually dressed employees are better workers because people are more productive when they're comfortable.

"I think Charlie is taking Casual Fridays a bit too far!"

SOURCE: www.CartoonStock.com

4 Now summarize the opinions in Exercise 3. Complete each statement below with a quantifier from the box.

each	several	half of	two	a number of
every	three	many	most	a couple of
some	four	one	a few	a majority of

1. _____ person expressed an opinion about business casual dress.

2. _____ people think business casual is a good idea.

3. _____ people think business casual is a bad idea.

4. _____ people think that dress and behavior are related.

5. _____ person thinks business casual is annoying.

5 Now rewrite statements 1–4 from Exercise 4, using different quantifiers with similar meanings.

1. _____

2. _____

3. _____

4. _____

Challenge. Judging from the statements in Exercise 3, do you think casual business dress is on the way out? _____

LESSON 2

6 **What Do You Think?** Comment on each of the fashions shown. Use the adjectives listed or your own adjectives. Where possible, use two adjectives.

chic	elegant	flashy	old-fashioned	sloppy	tacky
classic	fantastic	in style	out of style	striking	tasteful
eccentric	fashionable	loud	shocking	stylish	trendy

①  ②  ③  ④

1. *These pearls are elegant and chic.*   **3.** ....

2. ....   **4.** ....

⑤  ⑥  ⑦  ⑧

5. ....   **7.** ....

6. ....   **8.** ....

7 **Match each word or expression with its opposite. Write the letter on the line.**

1.	conform	**a.**	tacky
2.	classic	**b.**	subdued
3.	elegant	**c.**	trendy
4.	flashy	**d.**	cheap
5.	fashionable	**e.**	stand out
6.	shocking	**f.**	tasteful
7.	well made	**g.**	old-fashioned

In the summer of 2005, both the Japanese and Chinese governments asked office workers to dress down to save energy. A majority of Japanese companies complied with the "Cool Biz" no-tie, no-jacket campaign to reduce air-conditioner use. In Japan, about 210 million kilowatt hours of electricity were saved, reducing carbon dioxide emissions by about 79,000 tons.

SOURCE: www.japantimes.co.jp

8 List an article of clothing, a pair of shoes, or an accessory you have that can be described by each adjective.

   1. Trendy: ....

   2. Elegant: ....

   3. Striking: ....

   4. Out of style: ....

   5. Comfortable: ....

   6. Classic: ....

9 Challenge. Read the quote from 1930s fashion designer Elsa Schiaparelli. Then answer the questions.

> " Ninety percent [of women] are afraid of being conspicuous and of what people will say. So they buy a gray suit. They should dare to be different. "

   1. Rewrite Ms. Schiaparelli's fashion advice in your own words.

   ....

   ....

   2. Do you think this is good fashion advice for people (not just women) today? Why or why not?

   ....

   ....

LESSON 3

10 Think about people you know—friends, relatives, classmates, colleagues, etc. Write statements about things they do to make themselves more attractive. Use quantifiers and ideas from the box or your own ideas.

body piercing	hair coloring	nail extensions
braids	hair transplants	permanents
contact lenses	hair removal	sideburns
cosmetic surgery	long hair	skin tanning
facials	makeup	tattoos
false eyelashes	manicures	

Several men I know have long hair.

....

....

....

....

11 **Answer the questions.**

1. Do you think that most people are happy with their appearance, or that a majority would like to change their appearance?

2. What would you consider doing to change your appearance?

3. How far is too far? Which ways of changing one's appearance do you think are inappropriate, tacky, or shocking?

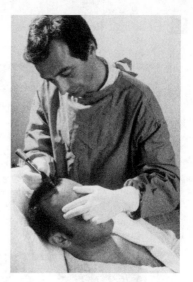

LESSON 4

12 **Reading Warm-up.** **Look at the ad. Then answer the questions.**

1. How would you describe the man in this ad?

2. Do you think that the man in this ad reflects how most men look?

3. Do you think men are more or less self-conscious about how they look than women are?

IN AS LITTLE AS 2 WEEKS

BUY NOW!!!
Limited time offer.
No more sit-ups!
CALL NOW!

Boys and Body Image

Most people realize that unrealistic ideals of beauty in the media have negatively affected the body image of women and girls. However, not as many are aware of the pressure on men and boys to conform to an ideal body type that television, movies, and magazines have started to define for them. Males are becoming more self-conscious and self-critical. They compare themselves to media images of muscular, well-built men and are not satisfied with how they look.

Half man and half god, Adonis was considered the ideal of masculine beauty by ancient Greeks.

The trend in advertising to use the male body to sell a variety of products—from clothes to exercise equipment—has led to an increase in negative body image and low physical self-esteem among men and boys. Although the majority of teenagers with eating disorders are girls, researchers believe that the number of boys affected is increasing. Also, like girls, teenage boys who think they're overweight are more likely to try smoking as a way to lose weight.

This new ideal of male beauty has also created some problems that are unique to men and boys. In an effort to attain the muscular bodies of the shirtless men in ads, many are turning to obsessive exercising and weight lifting. In the United States, the number of men who exercise has increased more than thirty percent since the start of the 1990s. While exercise is, of course, a healthy habit, exercising excessively is not. Some men spend so many hours at the gym that they don't have time for family and friends.

Researchers have defined a new body-image disorder, termed muscle dysmorphia, that is the reverse of the extreme dieting that has been a problem among girls and young women. Men with this disorder worry that they are too thin and small. As a result, they engage in extreme exercise and use a variety of products that promise bigger muscles and more energy. Some of these products—such as anabolic steroids—are dangerous. Abuse of these muscle-building drugs can cause serious health problems such as heart disease, liver cancer, and depression.

Research has shown that Western men are much more concerned with looking muscular than Asian men. Steroids are available legally and without a prescription in Beijing, but steroid abuse is generally not a problem in China. According to researcher Harrison Pope of Harvard University, "the Chinese idea of masculinity has more to do with inner strength—strength of character and intellect."

Sources: www.mediascope.org, www.infoplease.com, www.healthyplace.com

Now complete the statements with words from the box.

1. Advertisers use images of .... men to sell their products.

2. These images of perfect male bodies are an .... ideal.

3. They have caused many men to become more ....

4. As a result, a lot of men now suffer from low ....

5. Some of these men try to improve their appearance in ways that are ....

dangerous
self-esteem
muscular
unrealistic
self-conscious

14 **Answer questions about the article.**

1. According to the article, where do we see images that now define male beauty? ....

....

2. How has the modern ideal body type affected Western men's self-image? ....

....

3. What problems are some men having as a result? _____

_____

4. What do you think Western men could learn from Chinese men about self-image? _____

_____

Grammar Booster

A **Read each statement. Check the meaning of the quantifier in each sentence.**

	Some	Not many / Not much
1. Few people were dressed appropriately for the event.	☐	☐
2. There are a few really good books on fashion here.	☐	☐
3. I've got a little money put away for a rainy day.	☐	☐
4. I have little interest in pop music.	☐	☐
5. There are few hairstyles that look good on me.	☐	☐
6. There's a little cake left, if you'd like a piece.	☐	☐

B **Add _of_ to the sentences that need it.**

               of

1. Several ⌃ his co-workers wear suits to work.

2. A few friends are coming over for dinner on Friday night.

3. A few my friends are going to a movie tonight.

4. Both dresses look great on you.

5. A majority people still dress up to go to the theater.

6. This is the most traffic I've ever seen on this road.

7. Each the employees voted on whether or not to dress down on Fridays.

C **Complete each sentence with a phrase from the box. Change the verb as necessary to agree with the subject.**

be quite good	have tattoos	wear contact lenses
be self-confident	dress casually	

1. Most of my friends _____ .

2. A lot of pop music _____ .

3. Several of my classmates _____ .

4. One of my family members _____ .

5. None of the people I know _____ .

Writing: Compare ways people make themselves more attractive

A **Prewriting.** **Organizing ideas.** Choose one of the topics from the box.

> • Compare and contrast what you and someone you know well do
>   to make yourselves more attractive.
>
> • Compare and contrast what people today do to make themselves
>   more attractive with what they did twenty years ago.
>
> • Compare and contrast what celebrities do to make themselves
>   more attractive with what average people do.

Complete the diagram below. Label the circles with the people you're comparing. Think about
what people do (or did) to make themselves more attractive. List the differences in each circle
and the similarities in the middle.

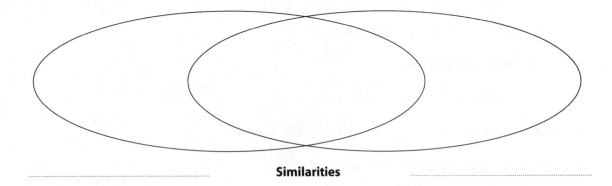

Similarities

B **Writing.** Write two paragraphs comparing and contrasting ideas within the topic
you chose, referring to your notes in the diagram.

> • In your first paragraph, write about the similarities. Remember to use connecting words such as
>   <u>like</u>, <u>similarly</u>, <u>likewise</u>, <u>as well</u>, and <u>not either</u>.
>
> • In your second paragraph, write about the differences. Remember to use connecting words such as
>   <u>unlike</u>, <u>in contrast</u>, <u>however</u>, and <u>whereas</u> / <u>while</u>.

....

....

....

....

....

....

....

....

C **Self-Check.**

☐ Did you correctly use connecting words for comparing?

☐ Did you correctly use connecting words for contrasting?

☐ Does each paragraph have a topic sentence?

UNIT 5

Community

PREVIEW

1 Think about a city you have lived in or visited. Then complete the chart with your opinions.

City: _____	
Things you like about the city	
Things you dislike about the city	
Trends (general changes taking place) in the city	
Things that could be done to improve life in the city	

2 Read the e-mail message.

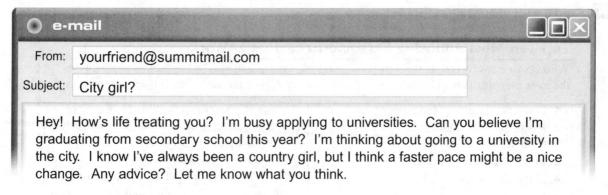

From: yourfriend@summitmail.com

Subject: City girl?

Hey! How's life treating you? I'm busy applying to universities. Can you believe I'm graduating from secondary school this year? I'm thinking about going to a university in the city. I know I've always been a country girl, but I think a faster pace might be a nice change. Any advice? Let me know what you think.

Now respond to the e-mail message. Do you think a move to the city is a good idea? Explain your opinion. Describe some advantages and disadvantages of life in the city. If you can, give advice on living in a city.

To: yourfriend@summitmail.com

Subject: RE: City girl?

LESSON 1

3 Combine each pair of sentences, using a possessive with a gerund.

1. He sleeps in class. What do you think about it?

   What do you think about his sleeping in class?

2. Julie's husband checks his PDA constantly. She can't stand it.

3. Patricia's co-workers call her Patty. She resents it.

4. They complain all the time. I'm so tired of it.

5. We take calls during dinner. Our father objects to it.

6. I hum while I work. Do you mind?

7. You are late so often. Mr. Yu objects to it.

4 Read the list of annoying office behaviors.

Top Ten Most Annoying Personal Behaviors at Work

What do your co-workers do that gets on your nerves? We recently asked our readers to e-mail us the most annoying personal behaviors of their officemates. Here are the ten most popular responses:

1. Chewing, smacking, and popping gum
2. Humming, whistling loudly, or listening to the radio in a shared work area
3. Interrupting conversations
4. Smoking at work
5. Inappropriate jokes, language, or comments
6. Inappropriate dress — either too casual or too shocking
7. Looking at the clock or at one's watch repeatedly during a meeting
8. Wearing too much perfume or cologne
9. Playing with objects on someone else's desk
10. Gossiping and complaining constantly

SOURCE: www.bizjournal.com

Now answer the questions.

1. Which behavior from the list do you find most annoying?

2. Can you think of any annoying workplace behaviors that aren't on the list?

3. Do you know someone who engages in one of these behaviors? How do you feel about it? Write a sentence, using a possessive with a gerund.

4. Write a sentence asking for permission to do one of the things listed.

5. Write a sentence politely asking someone not to do one of the things listed.

5 Judge the appropriateness of each behavior below. Write sentences, using adjectives from Student's Book page 53 or your own adjectives.

1. Using a hand-held phone while driving: *It's unsafe to use a hand-held phone while driving.*

2. Taking a call in a movie theater: _____

3. Turning your cell phone off in class: _____

4. Having a loud, personal conversation on the train: _____
_____

5. Talking on the phone while shopping: _____

6. Turning your phone to silent mode in a restaurant: _____
_____

7. Leaving your phone on during a flight: _____

Cell-phone use at public cultural events — such as plays, movies, concerts, and art exhibits — is now against the law in New York City. The penalty for violating the law is a fifty-dollar fine and removal from the theater, museum, etc. The law was passed in 2003 after two famous actors reacted to cell-phone users during Broadway performances. In mid-performance, Kevin Spacey turned to a member of the audience who had answered a cell phone and said, "Tell them you're busy." Laurence Fishburne wasn't as polite. When an audience member answered a phone during one of his performances, he yelled, "Turn your @#?!* phone off!"*

SOURCES: www.wired.com, www.playbill.com

LESSON 2

6 Offer acceptable alternatives for each inappropriate behavior. Use <u>either . . . or</u>.

1. Littering: *People should either throw their garbage in a trash can or hold on to it until they find one.*

2. Talking during a movie: _____

3. Playing loud music on a bus: _____

4. Gossiping: _____

5. Eating in class: _____

7 Rewrite each sentence, using <u>neither . . . nor</u> and the antonym of the adjective.

1. Listening to loud music and getting in and out of your seat constantly are inconsiderate on a flight. *Neither listening to loud music nor getting in and out of your seat constantly is considerate on a flight.*

2. Leaving a cell phone on and putting your feet up on the seat in front of you are discourteous in a movie theater. _____
_____

3. Talking on a cell phone and smoking while driving are irresponsible. _____
_____

4. Talking or laughing while the teacher is talking is disrespectful. _____
_____

5. Touching the art and taking flash photography in a museum are inappropriate. _____
_____

---

* Symbols such as @#?!* are used to politely denote curse words.

8 Read the pet peeves of visitors to a website.

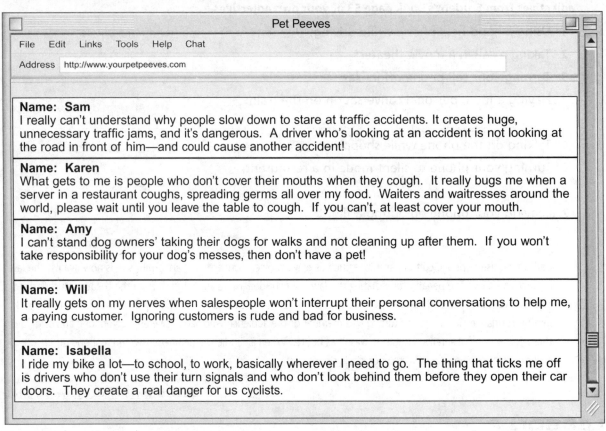

Pet Peeves

File   Edit   Links   Tools   Help   Chat

Address   http://www.yourpetpeeves.com

Name: Sam
I really can't understand why people slow down to stare at traffic accidents. It creates huge, unnecessary traffic jams, and it's dangerous. A driver who's looking at an accident is not looking at the road in front of him—and could cause another accident!

Name: Karen
What gets to me is people who don't cover their mouths when they cough. It really bugs me when a server in a restaurant coughs, spreading germs all over my food. Waiters and waitresses around the world, please wait until you leave the table to cough. If you can't, at least cover your mouth.

Name: Amy
I can't stand dog owners' taking their dogs for walks and not cleaning up after them. If you won't take responsibility for your dog's messes, then don't have a pet!

Name: Will
It really gets on my nerves when salespeople won't interrupt their personal conversations to help me, a paying customer. Ignoring customers is rude and bad for business.

Name: Isabella
I ride my bike a lot—to school, to work, basically wherever I need to go. The thing that ticks me off is drivers who don't use their turn signals and who don't look behind them before they open their car doors. They create a real danger for us cyclists.

Now rate the pet peeves according to how annoying they are to you. Number them
from 1 (most annoying) to 6 (least annoying).

.... drivers who slow down to stare at traffic accidents

.... servers who don't cover their mouths when they cough

.... dog owners who don't clean up after their dogs

.... salespeople who don't interrupt their personal conversations to help you

.... drivers who don't use their turn signals

.... drivers who don't look behind them before they open their car doors

9 **Challenge.** **Now read the pet peeves in Exercise 8 again. Write a sentence
summarizing each person's opinion. Use the paired conjunctions in parentheses.**

1. Sam's opinion (not only . . . but also): *Not only does slowing down to stare at traffic*
   accidents create huge, unnecessary traffic jams, but it's also dangerous.

2. Karen's opinion (either . . . or): ....

   ....

3. Amy's opinion (either . . . or): ....

   ....

4. Will's opinion (not only . . . but also): ....

   ....

5. Isabella's opinion (neither . . . nor): ....

   ....

10 **What About You?** **What's your pet peeve? Post a message to the message board. Use the messages in Exercise 8 as a guide.**

_____

_____

_____

_____

LESSON 3

11 **Check the community service activities that you or someone you know has done.**

☐ plant flowers or trees   ☐ collect signatures

☐ pick up trash   ☐ volunteer

☐ mail letters   ☐ make arrangements to donate your organs

☐ make phone calls   ☐ donate money

☐ raise money   ☐ other: _____

Now write sentences.

Example: Write about two activities you or someone you know has done. Use <u>not only</u> . . . <u>but also</u>.

Not only have I raised money, but I've also volunteered.

1. Write about two activities you or someone you know has done. Use <u>not only</u> . . . <u>but also</u>.

_____

2. Write about two activities you haven't done. Use <u>neither</u> . . . <u>nor</u>.

_____

3. Write about two activities you'd like to do. Use <u>either</u> . . . <u>or</u>.

_____

12 **Reading Warm-up. Describe your ideal vacation. Where would you go? What would you do? Where would you stay?**

13 Reading. **Read about the service organization started by husband and wife Bud Philbrook and Michele Gran.**

Bud Philbrook and Michele Gran were married in 1979. Instead of taking a honeymoon cruise to the Caribbean, they decided to spend a week in a rural village in Guatemala, where they helped raise money for an irrigation system. When they returned to their home in St. Paul, Minnesota, USA, the local newspaper wrote a story about their unusual honeymoon. Soon, people started contacting them, asking how they could plan a similar trip. Philbrook said, "We knew there was a need in rural communities around the world, and now we were learning people wanted to do this."

In 1984, the couple founded Global Volunteers, a nonprofit agency for people who want to spend their vacation helping others. Now the organization sends about 2,000 people each year to community development programs in twenty countries on six continents. These short-term volunteer service projects are focused on helping children and their families.

Volunteers are invited by local community leaders to work on projects that community members have identified as important. Not only do volunteers work side by side with local people, but they also live in the community. In most cases, no special skills are required. Anyone who wants to be of service and to learn about other cultures can volunteer. Global Volunteers' working vacations are popular with people of all ages. There are young, single volunteers and retired volunteers.

More recently, Global Volunteers has started offering programs for families with children as young as five. Some Global Volunteers community service opportunities include:

- helping to build clinics and community centers in mountain villages in Costa Rica.
- caring for infants with special needs in a rural hospital in Romania.
- working with orphaned and abandoned children in India.
- teaching conversational English in a large city or rural village in China.

SOURCE: www.globalvolunteers.org

Now answer questions about the article.

1. Where did Bud Philbrook and Michele Gran go on their honeymoon? ....

2. What did they do? ....

3. Why do you think they decided to spend their honeymoon in this way? ....

....

4. What effect did their story have on some people who read it? ....

....

5. What did Bud Philbrook and Michele Gran do as a result of people's interest in their trip?

....

14 What About You? **Would you consider a volunteer vacation? Answer the questions.**

1. In my opinion, a volunteer vacation would be ....

   a. a life-changing experience   c. more trouble than it's worth

   b. an adventure   d. kind of scary

   Explain your answer: ....

2. Some Global Volunteers live with local families. How comfortable would you be doing the same thing?

   a. very comfortable   **c.** a little uncomfortable

   b. somewhat comfortable   **d.** very uncomfortable

   Explain your answer: ....

3. At what stage in your life would you want to go on a volunteer vacation?

   a. young and single   **c.** married with a family

   b. married without kids   **d.** retired

   Explain your answer: ....

4. Which of the community services listed in the article would you want to do? Why?

   ....

5. Would you prefer to volunteer in a rural area or in a city? Why? ....

   ....

LESSON 4

15 **Reading. Look back at *The Advent of the Megacity* on Student's Book page 58. What is Dr. Perlman's opinion of planned cities?**

....

Now read about Canberra, Australia.

Canberra: A Planned City

Are planned cities too sterile? Not according to most people who live in or visit Canberra, Australia. With a population of just over 323,000, it's not a megacity—but it is Australia's largest inland city and its capital. Opinions of the entirely planned city cite plenty of pros and not a lot of cons. According to the travel guide Lonely Planet, it's "a picturesque spot with beautiful galleries and museums, as well as excellent restaurants, bars, and cafes."

One of the world's greenest cities, Canberra is surrounded by nature reserves, and a great deal of city land was set aside for parks and gardens. Canberra is proof that—with proper planning—the environment can be preserved in densely populated cities and towns.

Canberra also has excellent infrastructure. With wide roads that use roundabouts, rather than traffic lights, to regulate the flow of traffic, the city offers the shortest average commute times in Australia. Most city roads also have bike lanes, making cycling an important form of transportation in Canberra.

As a result of careful planning, Canberra offers the benefits of city living without the urban problems such as pollution and traffic. Not only does Canberra have clean air and water and good roads, but it also has affordable housing (cheaper than Sydney or Melbourne) and an abundance of health-care facilities. As the seat of Australia's government, Canberra has low unemployment and high education and income levels. It is a relatively safe city, with no murders reported in the 1999/2000 financial year. Canberra shows that planned cities can be great places to live and work.

Sources: www.up.edu.ph, www.education.nationalcapital.gov.au

16 Look back at the reading on page 45 and mark each statement about Canberra
True or **False**. Provide information from the article to support your choice.

    True False

1. ☐   ☐   Canberra suffers from a lack of culture and entertainment. ....

    ....

2. ☐   ☐   Transportation is a problem in Canberra. ....

    ....

3. ☐   ☐   Canberra has high levels of pollution. ....

    ....

4. ☐   ☐   Housing is not a problem for most people in Canberra. ....

    ....

5. ☐   ☐   A high percentage of people in Canberra cannot find work. ....

    ....

6. ☐   ☐   Crime is low in Canberra. ....

    ....

17 List one aspect of life in Canberra that appeals to you. Explain your answer.

....

....

18 **Challenge.** If you were going to design a city, what would be important
to you? Choose three urban problems from the box. Provide ideas about
how each problem might be prevented or alleviated through planning.

crime	corruption	disease	discrimination
overpopulation	pollution	poverty	inadequate public transportation
lack of housing	unemployment	other:	

Problem	Ideas
Unemployment	*Job training, encourage employers to locate in city*
1.	
2.	
3.	

> Hippodamus, a Greek architect of the 5th century B.C., is often considered the father of
> city planning. He designed the city of Miletus, using a grid plan for the layout of streets.
> (A grid is a pattern of straight lines that cross each other and form squares.)

SOURCE: www.wikipedia.org

Grammar Booster

A **Rewrite each sentence, using the word in parentheses. Make verb changes as necessary.**

1. John Coltrane was a great jazz musician, and so was Miles Davis. (too)

   John Coltrane was a great jazz musician, and Miles Davis was too.

2. The restaurant doesn't allow smoking, and neither does the bar. (not either)

3. Her company has adopted a casual dress code on Fridays, and his has too. (so)

4. Shorts aren't appropriate in the office, and neither are jeans. (not either)

5. She was annoyed by his behavior, and we were too. (so)

6. We've decided to volunteer, and so have they. (too)

7. Dave Clark doesn't like the city, and we don't either. (neither)

8. We're not going on vacation this summer, and they're not either. (neither)

B **Use the diagram below to compare two cities that you know. Consider things like traffic, weather, population, natural setting, architecture, infrastructure, and tourist attractions. Write similarities where the circles overlap and differences in the areas that do not overlap.**

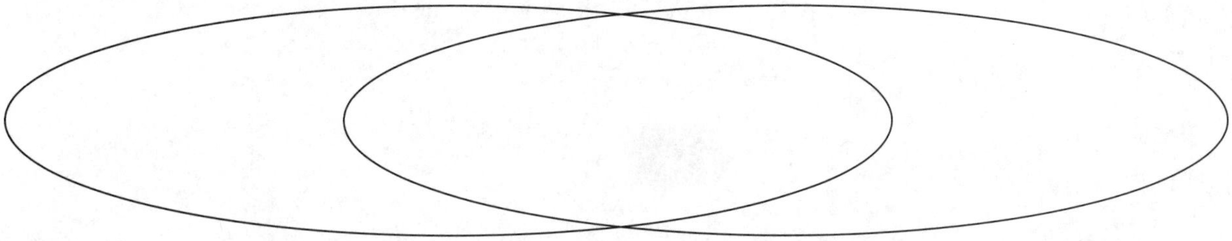

City: _____   Similarities   City: _____

Now use the information from the diagram to write sentences about ways in which the two cities are similar. Use conjunctions with <u>so</u>, <u>too</u>, <u>neither</u>, and <u>not either</u>.

1. _____
2. _____
3. _____
4. _____
5. _____

C Use short responses with <u>so</u>, <u>too</u>, <u>neither</u>, or <u>not either</u> to agree with the statements.

1. **A:** I don't really like the fast pace of life in the city.

   B: ....

2. **A:** I'm really annoyed by smoking in restaurants.

   B: ....

3. **A:** I try to be courteous about using my cell phone.

   B: ....

4. **A:** I can't understand why people talk during movies.

   B: ....

5. **A:** I speak up when something bothers me.

   B: ....

6. **A:** I don't have time to get involved with my community.

   B: ....

7. **A:** I would consider donating my organs.

   B: ....

Writing: An e-mail letter to an international website

A **Prewriting. Listing ideas.** Think about how visitors to your country generally behave, both positive and negative aspects. List reasons why their behavior is either positive or a problem. If it is a problem, list how you would like behavior to change.

....
....
....
....
....
....
....
....
....
....
....

http://www.GlobalCourtesy.com/soundoff

I am writing to complain about tourists' littering in our country. Not only is it inconsiderate, but it also detracts from the ability of everyone—tourists and locals alike—to enjoy all that our country has to offer.

Tourists come to our country from all over the world to enjoy our beaches, museums, and monuments. I have noticed many of them throwing candy wrappers, cigarette butts, and other things on the ground, rather than in trash cans. It is rude for them to expect the people who live here to clean up after them.

I urge all tourists who visit our country to please be considerate of your hosts and to clean up after yourselves. That way we can all enjoy your visit.

Sincerely,
Sasha Pilcher

B **Writing.** Use your notes to write an e-mail letter to an international tourism website. Remember to state how you feel about the behavior and, if appropriate, how you would like behavior to change.

....
....
....
....
....
....
....
....
....
....

C **Self-Check.**

☐ Did you use the proper salutation and closing?

☐ Are the tone and language in the letter appropriate for the audience?

☐ Did you use regular spelling and punctuation and avoid abbreviations?

Animals

PREVIEW

1 **Answer the questions.**

1. Write your own description of your personality. Refer to Student's Book page 62 for adjectives if you need to. ....
   ....

2. If you had to pick any animal to match your personality, what animal would it be?
   ....

3. What characteristics do you and this animal share? ....
   ....

2 **Match each animal with the adjective that best describes it.**
Write the letter on the line.

a. strong

b. quiet

c. brave

d. hairy

e. blind

f. slow

g. fat

h. playful

1. .... a bat

2. .... an ox

3. .... a mouse

4. .... a kitten

5. .... a lion

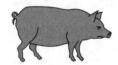

6. .... a pig

7. .... a gorilla

8. .... a snail

3 **A _simile_ is an expression that compares two things, using the words _like_ or _as_. Use your answers from Exercise 2 to write animal similes with _as_. Follow the example.**

1. _as blind as a bat_   5. ....

2. ....   6. ....

3. ....   7. ....

4. ....   8. ....

4 Look back at your answers in Exercise 1. Complete the sentence about yourself with a simile.

I'm ....

Now use some of the similes from Exercise 3 to describe people you know, famous people, or fictional characters.

1. *My mother-in-law is as blind as a bat.* ....
2. ....
3. ....
4. ....
5. ....

LESSON 1

5 Complete the sentences in the passive voice with <u>should</u> and a verb from the box. Some verbs will be used more than once.

allow	give	keep	protect	provide	treat

1. Animals on large farms .... humanely.
2. They .... with healthy food.
3. They .... with clean drinking water.
4. They .... to interact with other animals.
5. The animals .... space to move around.
6. They .... from predators.
7. They .... for illness or injury.
8. They .... comfortable in extreme weather.

6 In the following passive-voice sentences, use <u>can</u>, <u>can't</u>, <u>might</u>, <u>might not</u>, <u>shouldn't</u>, and <u>don't have to</u> with the verb in parentheses. Use each modal only once.

1. Dogfighting is illegal in all fifty U.S. states. Dogs .... for fighting in
   (raise)
   the United States.

2. Animals .... for sport or entertainment. Hunting, animal fighting,
   (harm)
   animal racing, and use of animals in circuses should be illegal in all countries.

3. Animals .... for their hides and fur. It's not necessary, because there
   (kill)
   are so many man-made materials that can keep people just as warm.

4. The cruel practice of testing cosmetics on animals .... if everyone
   buys only from companies that don't test on animals.   (eliminate)

5. Pets .... if there were more laws protecting them.
   (mistreat)

6. Alternatives to animal testing .... in the next decade.
   (develop)

7 What can be done to promote the humane treatment of animals? List some ideas.

_____

_____

LESSON 2

8 Reading. Read about the advantages and disadvantages of owning different popular pets.

FINDING THE BEST PET FOR YOU

Take time to learn all you need to know about the animal of your choice before bringing one home.

CATS

Cats are independent and easy pets to care for. And, as long as you aren't buying a purebred, they are economical pets, too.

Cats require little actual day-to-day care. They clean and groom themselves, tend to be self-reliant, and are usually happy to stay out of your way. But they can also be cuddly, playful, affectionate creatures—when they are interested.

Finding a kitten is usually easy, and they are often free.

DOGS

Dogs are generally eager to please, affectionate, and loyal, but they demand lots of time and attention. They need plenty of exercise and thrive on interaction with their owners. Daily walks, frequent baths, and feeding are a must.

Dogs range in price from free to quite expensive for some breeds. If you decide to buy a purebred, research the various dog breeds to find the best match for your household.

RABBITS

Rabbits love to run, are very sociable and intelligent, and most are quite adorable.

When deciding whether a rabbit is the pet for you, keep in mind that they require daily attention and care, much like dogs. A rabbit should get lots of exercise, live in a dry spot in your home, and get time out of its cage.

Rabbits are not costly to purchase or care for, though it's important to keep fresh hay and leafy greens on hand for them to eat.

HAMSTERS

Hamsters are easy pets for practically any family. They are amusing, affable, and cute. Hamsters have simple needs and are cheap to buy and to keep. Provide a dry living space outfitted with a gnawing log and a hiding place, and a hamster is content.

BIRDS

Birds have been blessed with lovely voices, though they are not quiet pets. Despite this, they are intelligent companions that are growing in popularity because they are pretty and quite independent.

Caring for birds is not difficult, but they do have special needs. They like to be active and to be challenged, and they must be housed in a place that is not too hot or too cold. Most love human interaction or other bird companions.

They should all be released from their cages periodically to explore their surroundings.

Birds can be quite costly to purchase, depending on which bird you buy, but the cost of caring for a bird is quite low.

SNAKES

If you're the average person, this is not the pet you want. Snakes require careful attention and owners with special knowledge to care for them.

Before you buy a snake, consider that it may grow up to weigh twice what you do and refuse to eat anything but live animals such as mice or insects, which you will need to provide. Temperature and lighting must be controlled, and the snake's enclosure must be secure.

Snakes range from being placid and docile to aggressive, depending on the individual snake. They can be fairly costly to purchase and to maintain.

FISH

Fish fit well in almost any type of household. They're quiet, generally peaceful, and, depending on your tastes, not expensive to buy or to shelter. Care is relatively simple and involves monitoring water and food.

Usually, the biggest expense involves an aquarium, some of which can be very expensive. For those who do not want exotic, pricey fish, a simple, adequately built aquarium will do and costs much less.

SOURCE: www.bankrate.com

Now complete the chart with information from the reading.

Pet	Personality traits	Care / special needs	Cost
Cats	independent, self-reliant	easy to care for	economical, often free
Dogs			
Rabbits			
Hamsters			
Birds			
Snakes			
Fish			

9 **Use information from the chart in Exercise 8 to answer the following questions.**

1. Which pets are low maintenance?

....

2. Which pets are high maintenance?

....

3. Which pets are costly to buy or care for?

....

4. Which pets are inexpensive to buy or care for?

....

5. Which pet would be best for your lifestyle? Explain.

....

....

Researchers have documented many health benefits associated with pet ownership. Owning a pet can help:

- reduce stress
- relieve loneliness and depression
- lower blood pressure
- prevent heart disease
- lower health-care costs
- stimulate exercise
- encourage laughter
- facilitate social contact

SOURCE: www.coloradan.com

Small dog breeds have become trendy in recent years. Celebrities such as Paris Hilton and Geri Halliwell are often spotted with their toy dogs tucked in their purses. As a result of this popularity, designer labels are selling high-end products for dogs—including clothes, collars, and jewelry.

SOURCE: www.coloradan.com

LESSON 3

10 Which character traits are positive? Which are negative? List each in the appropriate place.

| clever | gullible | mean | selfish | sincere | vain | wise |

Positive character traits

1. ....
2. ....
3. ....

Negative character traits

1. ....
2. ....
3. ....
4. ....

11 Answer the questions.

1. Who's the wisest person you know? What advice has he or she given you?

   ....

2. Describe a time when you did something clever.

   ....

3. Who do you think is a sincere politician?

   ....

4. What is the meanest thing someone has ever said to you?

   ....

5. What is one thing you could do to be less selfish?

   ....

12 Listen again to either the fable of "The Fox and the Crow" (Student's Book page 68) or "The Peacock's Tail" (page 69). Then write the story as well as you can from memory.

Did you know that *gullible* is the only word in the English language that's not in the dictionary? Go ahead, look it up.

If you looked it up, you are definitely gullible.

13 Reading. Read the fable of "The Stag with Beautiful Antlers." Then complete the card with information from the story.

ne morning a stag, drinking from a pond, saw his reflection in the water. He thought to himself, "What beautiful antlers I have. Don't I look elegant? But my skinny legs are a sorry sight in contrast! So spindly and bony."

The stag was still admiring his antlers when he heard the baying of hunters' dogs. He dashed away from the pond and ran to hide in the woods. His legs carried him swiftly and surely, but as he passed under a leafy tree, his antlers got caught in its branches.

The stag tried to free his antlers, but each time he shook his head, the more entangled he became. The dogs were getting closer. The stag gave one last, desperate tug and managed to free himself.

Once he was in the woods and able to catch his breath, he thought, "The antlers I admired so much nearly killed me, while the legs I hated so much saved my life."

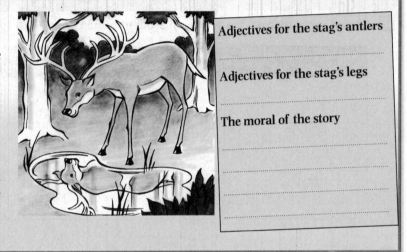

Adjectives for the stag's antlers
....

Adjectives for the stag's legs
....

The moral of the story
....
....
....
....

SOURCE: *Little Book of Fables* (Toronto: Groundwood Books, 2004)

14 Challenge. Complete each expression with the correct animal.

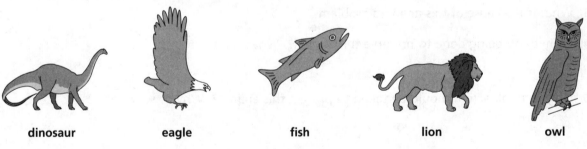

dinosaur   eagle   fish   lion   owl

1. A .... is something very large and old-fashioned that does not work well or effectively anymore.

2. To feel like a .... **out of water** is to feel uncomfortable because you are in an uncomfortable place or situation.

3. Someone who is ....-**eyed** is very good at seeing or noticing things.

4. A **night** .... is someone who enjoys staying awake late at night.

5. Someone who is brave is ....**hearted**.

15 Write your own sentences, using three of the animal expressions from Exercise 14.

Example: *I would feel like a fish out of water if I moved to the country.*

1. _____

2. _____

3. _____

LESSON 4

16 Use information from the article on Student's Book page 70 to complete the chart.

Animals at risk of extinction	Where they live	Problems affecting their habitats	The WWF's conservation efforts

17 Answer the questions.

1. Do you know of any other animal that is endangered or whose habitat is being destroyed?

_____

2. Where does this animal live? _____

3. What is the cause of this animal's problems? _____

4. Is anything being done to preserve this animal? What can be done? _____

_____

5. Do you think action should be taken to protect this animal? Why or why not? _____

_____

_____

According to The World Conservation Union, a total of 15,589 species of plants and animals are at risk of extinction. One in three amphibians and almost half of all freshwater turtles are threatened. Also, one in eight birds and one in four mammals are endangered.

Source: www.iucn.org

Grammar Booster

A **Circle the letter of the modal that best completes each sentence.**

1. I _____ have a pet parrot, but they require too much care.

   a. had better   **b.** would like to   **c.** am able to   **d.** should

2. If you don't mind, I _____ eat out tonight.

   a. wouldn't   **b.** don't have to   **c.** would rather not   **d.** must not

3. _____ Hillary play the violin well?

   a. Should   **b.** Must   **c.** May   **d.** Can

4. I'm sorry, but I _____ come to the meeting tomorrow.

   a. must not   **b.** won't be able to   **c.** couldn't   **d.** don't have to

5. Your sister's a tennis player? She _____ be very athletic.

   a. must   **b.** could   **c.** should   **d.** may

6. We _____ go skiing this weekend. We haven't decided yet.

   a. shouldn't   **b.** can't   **c.** had better not   **d.** might not

7. You _____ feed the animals—it's against the rules!

   a. don't have to   **b.** might not   **c.** had better not   **d.** aren't able to

8. I _____ take this class. It's required.

   a. may   **b.** could   **c.** have to   **d.** can

B **Complete each sentence with a modal. More than one answer may be possible in each sentence.**

1. You _____ turn on the TV while you wait, if you'd like.

2. It _____ snow tomorrow.

3. _____ I please borrow your pen for a moment?

4. If we leave at 4:00, there _____ be a lot of traffic.

5. We _____ check the weather before we go hiking.

6. If you don't want to see a movie, we _____ go out to eat instead.

7. My mother-in-law _____ have liked to go to Ireland, but she went to France instead.

8. He _____ have been very happy when he found out about his promotion.

9. You _____ smoke in this restaurant; it's prohibited.

10. He _____ come to the party last night because he had to work.

C **Complete each conversation in your own way. Use a modal.**

1. **A:** I passed Ellie on the street yesterday, and she didn't say hello.

   B: *She may not have seen you.*

2. **A:** It's too warm in here.

   B: ....

3. **A:** I don't feel like cooking tonight.

   B: ....

4. **A:** I don't know where to go on vacation this year.

   B: ....

5. **A:** Class was cancelled yesterday.

   B: ....

6. **A:** I've had this cold for three weeks now.

   B: ....

7. **A:** I'm a little hungry.

   B: ....

8. **A:** My brother wants to get a pet.

   B: ....

Writing: Express an opinion on animal conservation

A **Prewriting. Planning your argument.** Read the question below. State your opinion and list your arguments. Try to include examples, facts, or experts' opinions to support your opinion. Then list possible opposing arguments.

> **Is animal conservation important?**

Your opinion: ....

Your arguments	Possible opposing arguments
1.	**1.** ....
2.	**2.** ....
3.	**3.** ....

B **Writing.** Write a paragraph arguing your opinion from Exercise A. Remember to include a topic sentence at the beginning of the paragraph and a concluding sentence at the end.

....

....

....

....

....

....

....

....

....

....

....

C **Self-Check.**

☐ Did you state your point of view clearly?

☐ Did you provide examples, facts, or experts' opinions to support your point of view?

☐ Did you discuss opposing arguments?

☐ Did you include a topic sentence and a concluding sentence?

UNIT 7

Advertising and Consumers

PREVIEW

1 **Answer the questions.**

1. Do you have a favorite TV commercial, billboard, magazine ad, or radio ad?
   What product is it for? ....
   ....

2. Describe the ad. What type of ad is it? What do you like about it? ....
   ....
   ....

3. Do you use the product? Why or why not? ....
   ....

2 **What advertising have you been exposed to recently? List the brands or products you remember for each type of advertising.**

TV commercials: ....

Internet pop-ups: ....

Magazine ads: ....

Billboards: ....

Radio ads: ....

Ads on trains, buses, or blimps: ....

Now look at your lists. Which is the most effective way for advertisers to get their messages to you?

....

3 **Which expressions are positive reactions to a product? Which are negative? Check positive or negative.**

	positive	negative
1. Now that's something I'd like to get my hands on.	☐	☐
2. Sounds like a waste of money to me.	☐	☐
3. I think it could really come in handy.	☐	☐
4. You've got to be kidding.	☐	☐
5. What on earth for?	☐	☐

LESSON 1

4 Read each statement and then suggest the best place for each person to shop in your city or town. Use the vocabulary from Student's Book page 76.

I want to pick up some cheap sunglasses before we go sightseeing today. It would be a waste of money to buy designer ones. I'd just lose them!

I'd like to get some coffee, take a walk in this beautiful weather, and check out the new fall fashions.

1. *The open-air market on Fifth Street would be a good bet, if you don't mind haggling.*

2. ....
....
....

I've been saving up for a new digital camera. I'd like to check out a couple of different places before I buy one.

I don't really need anything, but I wouldn't mind just looking around. I actually find shopping relaxing.

3. ....
....
....

4. ....
....
....

5 Look online for something you're interested in buying. Record the prices you find on different websites. Comment on shipping costs, available brands, customer service, etc.

What are you shopping for? ....

Any particular brand? ....

Website: ....
Price: ....
Comments: ....

Website: ....
Price: ....
Comments: ....

Website: ....
Price: ....
Comments: ....

Which website has the best buy? ....

6 **Reading.** **Read the advice on shopping in Tokyo. Then complete the statements and answer the questions.**

TOKYO SHOPPING GUIDE

Below are descriptions of some of the best places to shop in Tokyo.

SOUVENIRS

"100-Yen" Shops
You can find 100-yen shops around many train stations and in some shopping areas. 100-yen shops are stores where most items cost 100 yen or less. In 100-yen shops, you can buy chopsticks, tableware, fans, kites, origami paper, calligraphy sets, "Hello Kitty" items, and much, much more! If you're looking for cheap souvenirs, 100-yen shops are the places to go.

Nakamise Shopping Arcade
This colorful, lively outdoor shopping street leads to the oldest temple in Tokyo. The walkway has been lined with souvenir shops

and local food stands for centuries. You'll find paper umbrellas, kimonos, rice cakes, sweets, and much more. Prices are, for the most part, reasonable.

Oriental Bazaar
Oriental Bazaar is the largest and most famous souvenir shop in Tokyo. It has four floors, and the higher you go, the more expensive the items get. Here you can satisfy all of your gift-giving needs at reasonable prices.

ELECTRONICS

Akihabara
Looking for the latest electronic gadgets? Check out the Akihabara district. It's the place to find the newest cell phones, TVs, *manga* anime CD-ROMs, even miniature robot pets. And it's one of the few places in Tokyo where you can try haggling.

CLOTHING AND ACCESSORIES

Ginza
The Ginza is a famous high-end shopping district in Tokyo. It's full of upscale department stores and expensive designer boutiques. The fashions tend to be more conservative here. For younger and trendier styles, go to Shibuya or Harajuku.

SOURCE: www.tokyoessentials.com

1. _____ are the best places to find inexpensive souvenirs in Tokyo.

2. Bargaining is generally not a part of Japanese shopping culture, but one place where it's acceptable is _____.

3. At _____, you might find a plastic samurai sword that's a steal in the basement and a traditional kimono that's a good deal on the top floor.

4. Prices are a bit steep here. If you're looking for a bargain, _____ is probably not the place to shop.

5. To pick up a few souvenirs, try some local snacks, and do a little sightseeing at the same time, _____ is a good bet.

6. Of the places listed in the guide, where would you be most interested in shopping? Why?
_____

7. Where would you like to browse? Why? _____

LESSON 2

7 Think of something that happened to you or that you heard about recently that blew you away, got on your nerves, cracked you up, or choked you up. What was it? Why did it make you feel that way?

....

....

....

8 Complete each sentence with the passive form of a gerund or an infinitive. Use verbs from the box.

ask	entertain	ignore	treat
call	force	inform	

1. Pam doesn't want .... about new products.

2. Alex can't stand .... by telemarketers.

3. I enjoy .... by funny commercials.

4. We hate .... to watch ads before movies.

5. I appreciate .... to join this company.

6. Scott hates ....

7. My daughter dislikes .... like a baby.

9 How do you feel about these forms of advertising? Write sentences with passive forms of gerunds or infinitives. Use verbs from the box or your own verbs.

can't stand	don't appreciate	like	prefer
dislike	don't like	love	resent

1. Spam: *I don't appreciate being sent e-mail ads that I don't want.* ....

2. Ads before movies: ....

3. Pop-up ads: ....

4. Direct mail: ....

5. Telemarketing calls: ....

6. Magazine ads: ....

7. Free product samples: ....

8. Product placement in movies: ....

LESSON 3

10 Complete each sentence with a word from the box.

| endorse | imply | promote | prove |

1. My kids are really going to want to get their hands on those sneakers now that their favorite baseball player has agreed to .... them.

2. I would buy the more expensive brand of toothpaste if the company could .... that it's more effective at fighting cavities.

3. I heard First Choice Pizza is giving away free slices tonight to .... its chain of restaurants.

4. The ads .... that their competitor's cars are unsafe.

11 Look again at the list of advertising techniques on Student's Book page 80. Can you think of ads that use these techniques? Complete the chart for as many of the techniques as you can.

> **In 1991, the Swedish government banned advertising directed at children under the age of twelve.**
>
> SOURCE: www.en.wikipedia.org

Advertising Technique	Product	How the technique is used
Example: Provide facts and figures	ZX-10 MP3 player	The manufacturer states how many songs it holds, how little it weighs, and how many hours it can play.
1. Provide facts and figures		
2. Convince people to "join the bandwagon"		
3. Play on people's hidden fears		
4. Play on people's patriotism		
5. Provide "snob appeal"		
6. Associate positive qualities with a product		
7. Provide testimonials		
8. Manipulate people's emotions		

Which of these techniques do you think is most effective? Why? ....

....

LESSON 4

12 **Reading Warm-up.** **Answer the questions.**

1. Do you enjoy shopping? ....

2. Do you feel comfortable shopping alone? ....

3. How often do you go shopping? ....

4. What do you buy for yourself? ....

5. Do you see a difference between men's and women's attitudes toward shopping?
....

13 **Reading.** **Read about the shopping habits of North American men.**

Shift in North American Men's Shopping Habits

According to a study commissioned by the men's magazine *GQ*, the shopping habits of North American men are changing significantly. In contrast to the traditional image of men as unwilling shoppers who aren't comfortable shopping for their own clothes, the new findings suggest that men now shop as a leisure activity, and that they make the majority of their own clothing purchases.

Men are becoming independent and more confident shoppers. They're well-informed, willing to shop alone, and no longer dependent on their wives, girlfriends, or sisters to make their purchasing decisions for them.

In addition, the study found that men shop more often than in the past and are increasingly likely to buy certain products for themselves—especially electronics, casual clothing, watches, and fragrance or grooming products.

Among the findings of the 2005 survey:
- 84 percent of men purchase their own clothes—compared with 65 percent in 2001.
- 52 percent of the surveyed stores reported having male customers who shop at least once a month—compared with 10 percent in 2001.
- Male customers shop at the surveyed stores an average of 18 times a year—compared with 5 times a year in 2001.
- Men's tendency to purchase products for themselves increased most for electronics (64 percent increase), casual clothing (62 percent), men's watches (53 percent), and fragrances/grooming products (50 percent).
- The average age of male apparel shoppers is 30–39.

Source: www.men.style.com

Now answer questions about the article.

1. According to the study, how are the shopping habits of North American men changing?
....
....

2. Do you think men's shopping habits are changing in a similar way in your country? Try to give examples to explain your answer.
....
....

3. Do you think the shift in men's shopping habits described in the article is a positive or a negative development? Explain your answer.
....
....

14 Reading Warm-up. **Answer the questions.**

1. What country do you think does the most online shopping? ....

2. What do you think is the most popular online purchase? ....

15 Reading. **Read about Internet shopping habits.**

Upward Trend in Global Online Shopping

According to a recent survey by AC Nielsen, more than 627 million people—one-tenth of the world's population—have shopped online. Books were the most popular purchase, with 212 million people reporting books as among the last three items they bought on the Internet. Books were followed by DVDs and video games, airline tickets, clothing/shoes/accessories, CDs and music downloads, electronic devices, computer hardware, and hotel reservations and tour bookings.

Among the 21,000 people from North America, Europe, Latin America, the Asia Pacific region, and South Africa who were surveyed, the Germans and the British turned out to be the world's most frequent online shoppers. In the month before the survey,

Germans made an average of seven purchases, Britons six. In general, European countries had the highest average purchases, followed by Canada and Asian Pacific countries, with an average of five. U.S. online shoppers made four purchases on average. Latin American shoppers made the fewest purchases, an average of three.

Why do European consumers shop online? One of the main attractions of Internet shopping for Germans is the ability to buy at any time of the day or night, as store hours in Germany are limited by law. British consumers similarly cite convenience, while Italians think online shopping is fun (according to a survey by GfK Ad Hoc Research Worldwide).

In countries with widespread Internet access, some reasons people give for *not* shopping online include the expense of surfing, nervousness about using credit cards online, worries about companies collecting information about their shopping likes and dislikes, and reluctance to purchase goods from retailers they don't know.

SOURCES: www.home.businesswire.com, www.clickz.com

Now answer the questions.

1. Were you surprised by the most popular online purchase? ....

2. Why do you think people buy more books than any other product online? ....

....

3. Do any of the reasons listed for <u>not</u> shopping online concern you? Why or why not? ....

....

16 Complete the chart by listing some advantages and disadvantages of shopping online.

Advantages	Disadvantages
It's easier to comparison shop.	

17 Check the items that you have purchased online.

☐ books   ☐ CDs or music downloads

☐ DVDs or video games   ☐ electronic devices

☐ airline tickets   ☐ computer hardware

☐ clothing / accessories / shoes ☐ hotel reservations or tour bookings

Now circle the items you've purchased in the last month. How many online purchases do you think you've made in the last month? ....

18 Answer the questions.

1. Describe consumer shopping habits in your country—including online shopping. Do you see differences between older and younger shoppers? Between women and men?

....

....

....

2. Describe your own shopping habits. Are you a compulsive shopper? Do you ever indulge yourself? How often? Do you ever make impulse buys, or do you wait and shop when there is a sale?

....

....

....

Grammar Booster

A Use the past gerund or infinitive form of the verbs in the box to complete the sentences. Use the passive voice where necessary. Refer to pages A3 and A4 in the Student's Book if you need to.

fool	have	sell
give	meet	steal

1. She was excited about _____ her favorite actor.
2. He was thrilled _____ the award.
3. I disliked _____ by that ad.
4. He admitted _____ money from the company.
5. She was pleased _____ the extra time to shop.
6. The store claimed _____ over 10,000 books that year.

B Combine each pair of sentences. Write one sentence, using a past form of a gerund or infinitive.

1. She was offered the position. She was pleased.

    She was pleased to have been offered the position.

2. He went to a conference last week. He mentioned it.

    _____

3. I wasn't told about the meeting. I resent it.

    _____

4. She missed the appointment. She made an excuse.

    _____

5. The manager gave the client the wrong information. The manager apologized.

    _____

6. She's finished her degree already. I didn't expect it.

    _____

7. He received a promotion. He was proud.

    _____

8. We missed the train. We had a good reason.

    _____

9. She used her corporate credit card for personal expenses. She was ashamed.

    _____

10. I was offended by her remarks. I pretended not to be.

    _____

Writing: Explain an article you've read

Choose one of the following articles to summarize:

- *Boys and Body Image*, Workbook page 36
- *Who Defines Beauty?* Student's Book page 46
- *Protecting Our Natural Inheritance*, Student's Book page 70
- An article you've read outside of class

A **Prewriting. Identifying main ideas.** Read the article you've chosen and underline or highlight the important parts. Then read the article again and list the main ideas below. (The article you have chosen may have fewer than six paragraphs.)

Main idea of paragraph 1:
Main idea of paragraph 2:
Main idea of paragraph 3:
Main idea of paragraph 4:
Main idea of paragraph 5:
Main idea of paragraph 6:

B **Writing**. Combine the main ideas to write your summary. Be sure to paraphrase what the author says, using your *own* words. Your summary should have one or two sentences for every paragraph in the original article.

....

....

....

....

....

....

....

....

....

....

Reporting verbs:	
argue	report
believe	say
conclude	state
point out	

Common expressions:
According to _____,
In _____'s opinion,
As _____ explains,
From _____'s point of view,

C **Self-Check.**

☐ Is your summary a lot shorter than the original article?

☐ Does your summary include only the author's main ideas?

☐ Did you paraphrase the author's ideas?

☐ Did you include your opinion of the article? If so, rewrite the summary without it.

Family Trends

PREVIEW

1 Read each situation. Then write a sentence summarizing what happened. Use one of the expressions from the box for each situation.

have a falling out	shape up	things work out
patch things up	talk back	

1. Last night after dinner I asked Jack to wash the dishes. He said, "No way, Mom. You wash the dishes." Can you believe he spoke to me like that?

....

2. Did you hear about the big fight Eva and Lana had? Lana got really upset, and they haven't talked for a couple of weeks now.

....

3. Tomas came over last night. When I opened the door, he handed me flowers and said, "I'm sorry, Rachel." We talked for a long time and realized that we'd both made mistakes.

....

4. Jason used to come in late and leave early, take long lunches, and miss meetings. Now he's here every morning at 7:00 on the dot, works late, and never misses a meeting. That talk with the boss must have really had an impact!

....

5. Anna and Mike Gunn had a difficult time making ends meet after Mike's accident. He couldn't go back to work. But now Anna has a job as a consultant, and Mike's a stay-at-home dad. They just bought a new car last week!

....

2 How can parents raise well-behaved kids who won't turn into troublemakers? Write sentences using <u>should</u> or <u>shouldn't</u>.

Should	Shouldn't
Kids should be given clear rules to follow.	*Kids shouldn't be criticized constantly.*

LESSON 1

3 Rewrite each sentence with a repeated comparative so that the sentence describes a trend. (Some sentences can be rewritten more than one way.)

1. People are moving to cities to find work.

   More and more people are moving to cities to find work.

2. People are spending long hours at work.

   People are spending longer and longer hours at work.

3. Men are getting involved in caring for their children.

   _____

4. People are spending time with their extended families.

   _____

5. Mothers are staying home to take care of their children.

   _____

6. Couples are choosing to remain childless.

   _____

7. Young adults are moving out of their parents' homes.

   _____

8. Adolescents receive adult supervision.

   _____

4 Complete the sentences, using double comparatives. Use the correct form of each word from the box.

develop	few	good	less	low	more

1. _____ people work, _____ time they spend with their families.

2. _____ a country is, _____ the healthcare system.

3. _____ the birthrate, _____ children there will be to care for older members of society.

few	good	high	long	more	old

4. _____ education you get, _____ your salary will be.

5. _____ the health-care system, _____ people live.

6. _____ people are when they get married, _____ children they are likely to have.

5 **Complete each double comparative. Use your own ideas.**

1. The longer I live, ...

2. The harder you work, ...

3. The more that you read, ...

4. The better I get to know people, ...

5. The more things change, ...

Now compare your sentences with these famous quotes.

"The longer I live, the more beautiful life becomes."
—**Frank Lloyd Wright,** architect
(1869 –1959)

"The harder you work, the luckier you get."
—**Samuel Goldwyn,** movie producer
(1882–1974)

"The more that you read, the more things you will know. The more that you learn, the more places you'll go."
—**Dr. Seuss,** children's book author (1904 –1991)

"The better I get to know men, the more I find myself loving dogs."
—**Charles de Gaulle,** French leader
(1890 –1970)

"The more things change, the more they are the same."
—**Alphonse Karr,** author
(1808 –1890)

Choose one of the quotes and describe what it means. How does it apply to your life and/or to the world today?

....

....

....

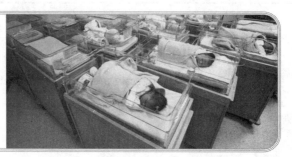

Of the 35 richest countries, in only three – Iceland, New Zealand, and the United States – are women having enough babies to replace the existing population.

Source: *The Economist,* Dec. 21, 2000

LESSON 2

6 What do you think parents should do if their teenaged kids start smoking?
Read each idea and decide how effective you think it would be.

Parents should . . .	ineffective	somewhat effective	very effective
accept that there's not much they can do.	O	O	O
talk to their kids about the health risks of smoking.	O	O	O
ask their kids questions to find out why they are smoking.	O	O	O
ground them.	O	O	O
let their kids know that they disapprove of their smoking.	O	O	O
talk to their kids about other negative effects of smoking, such as poor sports performance, smelly clothes and hair, bad breath, and yellow teeth.	O	O	O
allow their kids to make their own mistakes.	O	O	O
explain how the tobacco industry's advertising targets young people to become smokers.	O	O	O
have their kids visit people who have lung cancer.	O	O	O
not make a big deal about a little bit of rebellious behavior.	O	O	O
quit smoking themselves if they are smokers.	O	O	O

What do you think is the best idea? Why? ....

....

According to worldwide smoking statistics compiled by the World Health Organization:

- About one in five young teenagers (aged 13–15) smokes.
- Between 80,000 and 100,000 children, roughly half of whom live in Asia, start smoking every day.
- Around 50 percent of those who start smoking as adolescents go on to smoke for 15 to 20 years.
- Teenagers are heavily influenced by tobacco advertising.
- About a quarter of youth alive in the Western Pacific Region will die from the effects of smoking.

SOURCE: www.wpro.who.int

7 Read the teen blog entries and describe the teens' or their parents' behavior.
Use the vocabulary from Student's Book page 90.

Back | Forward | Reload | Stop | Home | Search

1. Posted: 10:09 AM

Princess5574
Hey! It's my birthday! When I woke up this morning, I went downstairs and opened the gifts my parents had left for me. I got some jewelry, some clothes, a new laptop – nothing special. I was a little disappointed. But when I walked out of the house, I found my real present in the driveway! My sports car – exactly the one I had asked for. I can't wait to drive it to my party on Saturday.

REPLY

2. Posted: 11:48 AM

Nolife312
They gave you a car? My parents won't even let me learn how to drive, or go anywhere in anyone else's car – or ride my bike down the street! I need to be able to hang out with my friends, go to the movies, maybe even go to a party every once in a while. I love my parents, but they're ruining my life!

REPLY

3. Posted: 1:02 PM

Norules721
Well, at least your parents care about what you do. My parents let me go where I want, do what I want, come home when I want. They don't mind if I invite the whole school over for a party. I know they love me, but I wish they would stop trying to be "cool" and act more like parents.

REPLY

---

1. *Princess is spoiled. Her parents are* ....

2. ....

3. ....

---

8 **What About You?** Check the sentences that describe your upbringing.

Lenient upbringing		Strict upbringing	
○	My parents did things for me that I could or should have done for myself.	○	My parents made me do many things for myself.
○	My parents did not expect me to do many chores or to help much around the house.	○	I had to do a lot of chores around the house.
○	I was allowed to have almost any clothes I wanted.	○	I had to use my own money to buy clothes.
○	My parents gave me too much freedom.	○	I wasn't given very much freedom.
○	My parents allowed me to take the lead or dominate the family.	○	My parents used physical punishment to discipline me.
○	My parents did not enforce their rules.	○	My parents set a lot of rules for me to follow.

Do you think you were spoiled as a child? Were your parents too strict? Or did you grow up with a nice balance between strictness and leniency? Explain and try to give examples.

....

....

....

What should parents do (or not do) to raise kids who aren't spoiled? List some ideas.

....

....

....

LESSON 3

9 Match the words with their definitions. Write the letter on the line.

1. .... frustration

2. .... involvement

3. .... courtesy

4. .... maturity

5. .... obedience

a. willingness to do what someone in a position of authority tells you to do

b. the quality of behaving in a sensible way and like an adult

c. the act of taking part in an activity or event, or the way in which you take part in it

d. the feeling of being annoyed, upset, or impatient, because you cannot control or change a situation or achieve something.

e. polite behavior that shows that you have respect for other people

10 Challenge. Circle the letter of the best choice to complete each sentence.

1. His parents intend for him to get married as soon as he finishes college. That is their ....

   a. explanation   b. importance   c. expectation   d. impatience

2. Carl Brooks is almost thirty-eight years old and still living in his parents' home. His parents resent his ....

   a. dependence   b. dependability   c. development   d. difference

3. Her parents don't think she should change jobs again. They worry about her long-term financial ....

   a. mobility   b. security   c. lenience   d. confidence

4. Dana Wolf doesn't like her daughter's new boyfriend. She thinks he's lazy and disrespectful. She can't understand her daughter's .... to him.

   a. attractiveness   b. consideration   c. involvement   d. attraction

Answer the questions.

1. What is a "generation gap"?

....

2. What developments (political, technological, social, etc.) do you think have contributed to the generation gap between your generation and that of your parents?

....

3. In what ways are your generation and that of your parents similar?

....

....

LESSON 4

12 **Reading Warm-up.** **How are the responsibilities of caring for children different from those of caring for the elderly? How are they the same?**

....

....

13 **Reading.** **Read the article.**

The Sandwich Generation

In the United States and Canada they've been termed the sandwich generation— people caught between the needs of their growing children and their aging parents, having to care for both. Factors giving rise to the sandwich generation include the fact that people are having children later in life, combined with longer life expectancies. Whatever the cause, this new responsibility places many demands on these caregivers' time and energy and leaves little space for attending to their own needs.

Some members of the sandwich generation are parents in their 30s or 40s caring for young children. For example, Pamela Bose, 40, has a three-year-old and a nine-year-old. She has recently taken over the care of her widowed mother. One minute she is worrying about getting the children to school on time; the next, she is checking to make sure that her mother has remembered to take her medicine. "I spend so much time keeping up with their competing demands that I end up not devoting enough time to anyone, let alone making time for myself," says Bose.

(continued on page 77)

The Sandwich Generation *(continued)*

Other members of the sandwich generation are parents in their 40s or 50s caring for teenaged or adult children. Nowadays more adult children are living at home while they're in college and even afterward, as they get established and figure out what they want to do. Also, an increasing number of adult children are returning home to live after a divorce or job loss.

The longer adult children remain dependent on their parents, the more people find themselves in the sandwich generation. Patricia Rivas is one of these people. She and her husband David both have careers. They have a teenaged son, a recently divorced daughter with a two-year-old child, and an elderly father who has early dementia and is requiring more and more care, all living in the same household.

Most sandwich-generation caregivers are women. Increased female labor-force participation means that many of these women are balancing not only care for their children and parents but also their own careers. Without a doubt, trying to meet all of these obligations at the same time is stressful. It's not surprising that sandwich-generation members report an increase in depression, sleeplessness, headaches, and other health problems. While many are happy about the chance to help care for their parents, they also feel guilty about not doing more.

As sandwich-generation members try to respond to everyone else's needs, it's important that they not ignore their own needs. As these caregivers struggle to give their young children attention and patience, their older children support and guidance, their elderly parents not only the physical care they need but also opportunities for social interaction and inclusion in family life, it is also important that they make some time for their own relaxation, something that is more often than not overlooked.

SOURCE: www.health24.com

Now answer the questions, using information from the article.

1. What is the "sandwich generation"?

   ....

2. How is the term "sandwich" appropriate to describe this generation?

   ....

3. Name three trends that are responsible for the development of the "sandwich generation."

   ....

   ....

   ....

4. What are some problems that sandwich-generation members experience?

   ....

   ....

5. Why is being a member of the sandwich generation especially stressful for women?

   ....

   ....

14 Look back at the article on pages 76–77. Find the nouns that correspond to the verbs and adjectives below. Write them on the lines.

1. responsible: ....

2. participate: ....

3. obligate: ....

4. depress: ....

5. sleepless: ....

6. patient: ....

7. guide: ....

8. interact: ....

9. include: ....

10. relax: ....

> Life expectancy in India and the People's Republic of China was around 40 years in the middle of the 20th century. By the end of the century, it had risen to around 63 years.
>
> **SOURCE:** www.en.wikipedia.org

> In the U.S., approximately 44 percent of people between the ages of 45 and 55 have children under 21 and also have aging parents or in-laws.
>
> **SOURCE:** www.imdiversity.com

15 Do you know anyone who is caring for their children and/or an elderly family member? Describe the person's situation. What challenges is he or she facing?

Grammar Booster

A Read each pair of statements. Then complete each sentence, using a comparative, superlative, or comparison with <u>as</u> . . . <u>as</u>.

1. Today's hike is 5 km. But our hike yesterday was 7 km.

   Today's hike is *shorter than yesterday's hike* .

2. A cheetah can run 96 km per hour. A greyhound can run 64 km per hour.

   A greyhound can't run _____ .

3. I am 24 years old. My brother is 20, and my sister is 18.

   Of the three of us, I am _____ .

4. Park City is 5 km from here. Greenville is 10 km from here.

   Greenville is _____ .

5. His parents are very strict. My parents are not very strict.

   My parents are _____ .

6. Mr. Plant has two children. Mr. Lane has four children.

   Mr. Plant has _____ .

7. I paint well. Ten years ago, I didn't paint well.

   I paint _____ .

8. There are five people in my family. There are five people in Irene Lee's family too.

   There are _____ .

9. My commute to work is 14 km. My colleague Mrs. Young has a 20 km commute, and my other colleague, Mr. Davis, travels 30 km to work.

   Of the three of us, I have _____ .

10. My grandmother is 80 years old. My grandfather is 78 years old.

    My grandfather isn't _____ .

B Compare people and things you know. Use comparatives or <u>as</u> . . . <u>as</u>.

Example: two friends—adventurous

   Megan is more adventurous than Matthew.

1. two friends—adventurous

   _____

2. two movies—funny

   _____

3. two books—long

   _____

4. two stores—expensive

   _____

5. two TV shows—good

   _____

(continued on page 80)

6. two singers—sing well

....

7. two family members—work hard

....

C Complete each statement. Use your own idea in the first blank and a superlative in the second.

1. *Liver* .... is *the worst* .... thing I've ever eaten.

2. .... is .... person I've ever met.

3. .... is .... place I've ever been.

4. .... is .... thing I've ever done.

5. .... is .... thing I've ever bought.

6. .... is .... thing I've ever said.

D Challenge. Read each sentence. Then write a sentence with similar meaning, using a comparative, a superlative, or as . . . as.

1. At 421 meters, the Jin Mao Building in Shanghai is very tall.

The Jin Mao Building in Shanghai is more than 400 meters tall.

2. The population of Greenland is only 59,827.

....

3. The movie we watched last night was so depressing.

....

4. Alexis McCarthy is becoming a very good violin player because she practices daily.

....

5. Sometimes he watches TV, but usually he reads.

....

6. The new French restaurant on City Avenue looks expensive, but it's really not.

....

Writing: *Compare your generation with that of another family member*

Choose a family member of a different generation from you, write about how your generations are different and how they are similar. (But, before you do, identify and correct the error in the previous sentence.)

A **Prewriting. Organizing ideas.** After you've chosen a family member of a different generation, label the circles in the diagram with your name and the family member's name. Then write differences between your two generations in each circle and similarities in the middle. Write quickly and don't worry about spelling, punctuation, etc.

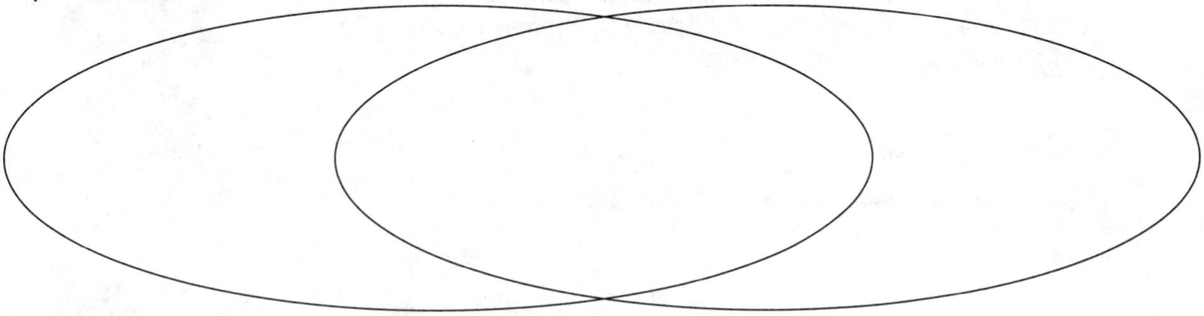

Similarities

B **Writing.** Write one or two paragraphs comparing the two generations you chose. Include a topic sentence that expresses your main idea. Avoid run-on sentences and comma splices.

C **Self-Check.**

☐ Did you write any run-on sentences? Comma splices? If so, correct them.

☐ Do all the sentences support the topic sentence?

☐ Are the paragraphs interesting? What could you add to make them more interesting?

History's Mysteries

PREVIEW

1 Read the stories below. Rate the probability that each is true.

1. A couple was on vacation in Australia, driving through the bush, when they accidentally hit a kangaroo. They decided to prop the kangaroo up and take a photo. To add a bit of humor, they dressed it up in the husband's jacket.

   As it turned out, the kangaroo was only stunned, not dead, and it hopped away with the jacket on. In the jacket pocket were the keys to their rental car and all their vacation money.

It's probably true.   It could be true.   I have no idea.   It can't be true.

2. A college student stayed up late studying for a math final exam. He overslept and arrived late for the test. He found three problems written on the board. He solved the first two pretty easily but struggled with the third. He worked frantically and figured out a solution just before the time was up.

   That night the student received a phone call from his professor, who told him that the third problem wasn't a test question. Before the test had started, the professor had explained that it was a problem previously thought to be unsolvable. But the student had solved it!

It's probably true.   It could be true.   I have no idea.   It can't be true.

3. A man was jogging through the park one day when another jogger lightly bumped him and excused himself. The man was just a little annoyed—until he realized that his wallet was missing. He immediately began chasing the jogger who'd bumped into him. He caught up to him and tackled him, yelling, "Give me that wallet!" The frightened "thief" handed over a wallet and quickly ran off.

   When the man got home, his wife asked him if he'd remembered to stop at the store. Anxious to tell his story, the man said that he hadn't, but that he had a good excuse. Before he finished, his wife said, "I know—you left your wallet on the dresser."

It's probably true.   It could be true.   I have no idea.   It can't be true.

SOURCES: www.warphead.com, www.snopes.com

2 Now put the conversation about the third story in order. Write numbers on the lines.

.... What? You've heard it before?

.... What happened?

.... It's a story that people pass on, about something unusual that happened to an ordinary person. A lot of people believe them, but they're usually not true.

1 You'll never guess what happened to a friend of a friend's husband.

.... Yeah, I have. The jogger took the other guy's wallet and then got home and realized he had left his wallet at home. It's an urban legend.

.... Wow. I had no idea. It seemed believable.

.... Well, he was jogging in the park, and this guy bumped into him. He thought the guy had stolen his wallet, so he chased him and tackled him . . .

.... What's an urban legend?

.... Don't tell me you buy that story!

3 Challenge. Do you know any urban legends or fantastic stories? Write one of them below.

....

....

....

....

....

LESSON 1

4 Read the questions below and answer the ones you can. If you don't know the answer, either guess (using <u>I'll bet</u> . . .) or use phrases from Student's Book page 100 to say that you don't know.

1. Is someone with a <u>sanguine</u> personality optimistic or pessimistic? ....

2. Who composed *Swan Lake*? ....

3. Who's the richest person in the world? ....

4. What is the French term for high fashion? ....

5. What city has the world's largest subway system? ....

6. How long does the average elephant live? ....

7. When was the first TV commercial broadcast? ....

8. What country has the highest life expectancy? ....

5 Report on each person's phone message. Use indirect speech. Follow the example.

"Hey. It's Jack. I'm stuck in traffic. I'll be there as soon as I can."

1. _Jack said (that) he was stuck in traffic and (that) he would be there as soon as he could._

"Hi. It's Melanie. I have another meeting at 8:30. I may be late."

2. _____

"Hi. This is Allison. I can't come in today. My son isn't feeling well."

3. _____

"Hello. It's Alex. I have to make some copies. I'll be there by 9:15."

4. _____

6 Read the situation below. Then, for each of the times listed, write a sentence about what could have happened. Use the vocabulary from Student's Book page 101.

Your friend was supposed to arrive on the 8:05 train. You are waiting outside the station, but she still isn't there.

Example: (8:10) Not certain: _Maybe she's getting her luggage._

1. (8:10) Not certain: _____

2. (8:15) Somewhat certain: _____

3. (8:20) Almost certain: _____

4. (8:35) Very certain: _____

LESSON 2

7 Read the statements and check whether each speaker is <u>not certain</u>, <u>almost certain</u>, or <u>very certain</u>. Then rewrite each sentence, using a perfect modal in the passive voice. Use the appropriate degree of certainty.

not certain   *almost certain*   *very certain*

1. ☑ ☐ ☐ It's possible that language was developed to allow humans to hunt in groups more effectively.

   Language may have been developed to allow humans to hunt in groups more effectively.

2. ☐ ☐ ☐ Maybe the dinosaurs were killed by climate changes.

3. ☐ ☐ ☐ Probably the giant stone statues on Easter Island were carved by the ancestors of the Polynesian people who live there today.

4. ☐ ☐ ☐ Most likely Amelia Earhart was killed when her plane ran out of fuel and went down in the Pacific Ocean.

5. ☐ ☐ ☐ Clearly the fire was started intentionally.

6. ☐ ☐ ☐ There's no question the ship was sunk by a collision with an iceberg.

8 Reading Warm-up. Look at the picture and caption. Then speculate about what happened to the *Mary Celeste*, using the perfect form of the modal <u>may</u> in the passive voice.

The *Mary Celeste* was discovered drifting off the coast of Portugal in 1872. There was no one aboard.

Example: *The crew may have been washed overboard by a giant wave.*

Your speculation: ....

9 **Reading.** Read more about the circumstances surrounding the disappearance of the *Mary Celeste*'s crew and passengers.

The *Mary Celeste*

On November 7, 1872, the *Mary Celeste* sailed under the command of Captain Benjamin Briggs—known as an honest and fair man. He, his wife, young daughter, and a crew of seven departed from New York City for Genoa, Italy, carrying a cargo of alcohol. They were never seen again.

On December 4, another ship spotted the *Mary Celeste* drifting off the coast of Portugal. A few men from the ship boarded the *Mary Celeste* to offer help. Although there was some damage, it was not extensive, and the ship was seaworthy. The cargo and a six-month supply of food and water were still on board the ship. However, nine of the 1,700 barrels of alcohol were empty, and the lifeboat and all of the passengers and crew were missing. The last entry in the logbook was dated November 24, 1872.

Many theories have been proposed to explain the mystery of the disappearance of the *Mary Celeste*'s crew and passengers. Here are some of them:

- The crew killed Captain Briggs and his family and escaped in the lifeboat.
- The nine barrels of alcohol had leaked. Afraid the fumes would cause an explosion, Captain Briggs ordered everyone into the lifeboat. The lifeboat got separated from the ship, and its occupants drowned or died at sea.
- A giant octopus snatched the crew one by one from the deck of the ship.

SOURCE: www.en.wikipedia.org

Now speculate about the probability of each theory explaining the disappearance of the *Mary Celeste*'s passengers and crew. Use perfect modals in the passive voice. Explain your answers.

1. The theory that the captain was killed by the crew:

   ....

   ....

2. The theory that the crew was forced by alcohol fumes to leave the ship:

   ....

   ....

3. The theory that the crew was snatched from the ship by a giant octopus:

   ....

   ....

LESSON 3

10 Write the words from the box in order from least certain to most certain.

| believable | debatable | provable | questionable | unsolvable |

Least certain ──○──────○──────○──────○──────○──→ Most certain

....

11 Use the words from Exercise 10 to complete the paragraph.

I recently received an e-mail message of _____ truthfulness. Of course,
1.
whether or not it's a good idea to even open these types of forwarded messages is

_____. However, I did open it. According to the e-mail story, a woman and
2.
her daughter had enjoyed a delicious cookie in the café of a high-end department store in
the United States. The cookie was so good that the woman asked for the recipe. The server
replied that woman could purchase the recipe for "two fifty." The woman agreed and
asked that the charge be added to her credit card bill. When the woman received her bill in
the mail, the charge for the cookie recipe was two hundred and fifty dollars—not two
dollars and fifty cents. I guess a lot of people must find this story _____,
3.
because the message keeps getting forwarded. Personally, I don't buy the story. Of course,
whether or not the story is true is not an _____ mystery. It's easily
4.
_____. All you would have to do is go to the store's café and ask to buy the
5.
cookie recipe—and pay in cash.

SOURCE: www.bl.net

12 Challenge. Have you received similar types of e-mail messages, or have you
ever heard a story that you thought was questionable? Write the story below.
How believable is it? Is it provable?

_____

_____

_____

_____

_____

LESSON 4

13 Reading Warm-up. Read the excerpt from the poem "The Puppet."

. . . if only I had a scrap* of life . . .
I wouldn't let a single day go by without
saying to people I love that I love them.

I would convince each woman [and] man that
they are my favorites, and I would live in
love with love.

*scrap = a small piece of something

Speculate about the poem's author. Check the statement that you think is most likely.

☐ The author is in love.

☐ The author is dying.

☐ Other: _____

Gabriel García Márquez's Final Message

A poem signed with Gabriel García Márquez's name appeared in the Peruvian newspaper *La República* on May 29, 2000. The title of the poem was "La Marioneta," or "The Puppet." The newspaper reported that García Márquez had written the poem and sent it to his closest friends as a way to say good-bye to them. Apparently, García Márquez's health was poor and he expected to die soon.

Other newspapers quickly picked up the story. On May 30, many Mexico City newspapers published the poem. The poem appeared on the front page of the Mexican newspaper *La Crónica.* The poem was superimposed on the author's photo, and the newspaper's headline read, "Gabriel García Márquez sings a song to life." The poem quickly spread throughout the world via the Internet. Many people who read the poem were deeply moved. For example, the Indian filmmaker Mrinal Sen told the *Hindustan Times* that,

after reading the poem, he was flooded with memories of his twenty-year friendship with García Márquez.

However, it soon became clear that Gabriel García Márquez was not dying. Although he had been treated for lymphatic cancer in the summer of 1999, the rumors about his failing health were not true. It also became clear that the sentimental poem was not the work of the Nobel-prize-winning author. The poem was actually written by a Mexican ventriloquist named Johnny Welch. He had written the poem for his puppet, "Mofles." No one is sure how his name was replaced by García Márquez's.

SOURCE: www.museumofhoaxes.com

Now answer questions about the article.

1. What did the newspaper articles claim about Gabriel García Márquez?

....

2. Which do you think is more likely: The newspapers looked for evidence of the poem's authenticity, or the newspapers rushed to print the poem?

....

3. Do you think Johnny Welch was a forger? Explain your answer.

....

4. If you'd read the story in *La República*, *La Crónica*, or the *Hindustan Times*, do you think you would have believed it?

....

15 Challenge. **How do you think the Internet has affected the spread of questionable claims and stories?**

....

....

....

Grammar Booster

A **Read the sentences. Then use <u>said</u>, <u>told</u>, or <u>asked</u> to rewrite each quote as indirect speech.**

1. Sonia: "Oh, Robert, I saw Paul at the supermarket."

   Sonia told Robert that she had seen Paul at the supermarket.

2. The salesperson: "Neil, the video cameras may go on sale tomorrow."

   ....

3. Stephen: "I have to work tonight."

   ....

4. Caroline: "Can I turn on the TV?"

   ....

5. Allen: "OK, kids, you have to clean up your toys."

   ....

6. Professor Johnson: "Class, did you complete the assignment?"

   ....

B **Rewrite the quotations as indirect speech. Use reporting verbs from the box. (You will not use all the reporting verbs.)**

add	answer	complain	explain	mention	remark	reveal
announce	comment	exclaim	maintain	promise	report	write

1. "The economy will improve."   —*The president*

   The president promised that the economy would improve.

2. "My client cannot be guilty of the charges."   —*The attorney*

   ....

3. "There is no scientific evidence of negative side effects."   —*Smith Pharmaceuticals*

   ....

4. "The earthquake has left one million people homeless."   —*The Daily Journal*

   ....

5. "We may have to lay off some employees."   —*Strauss-Lyon, Inc.*

   ....

6. "My team will make the championships this year!"   —*Coach Moore*

   ....

7. "There aren't enough services for poor families."   —*Anna Graham, Director of City Kids*

   ....

Writing: *Write about an interesting experience*

A Prewriting. Generating ideas with information questions.

Think about something interesting that you did or experienced in the past.
The experience you've chosen will be your topic. Write information questions
about the topic to help generate ideas.

Topic: _____

Who? _____

What? _____

When? _____

Where? _____

Why? _____

How? _____

_____

_____

WRITING MODEL

A New Friend

Last summer I made a new friend while on
vacation in Italy. I was hiking in a region
called Cinque Terre when I met a man
named Flavio. We discovered that we both
spoke English, and we began talking. We
got along so well that he invited me back
to his family's home for lunch. I met his
mother, father, and brothers and sisters. His
mother made a delicious lunch, and we ate
it in their beautiful home overlooking the
ocean. I spent a delightful afternoon with
Flavio and his family, and by the end of the
day we were friends. We still write to each
other, and I plan to visit again next year.

B Writing. Write about the experience, answering your
questions from Exercise A. Try to include as much information
as you can. Choose a title that reflects your main idea.

....

....

....

....

....

....

....

....

....

....

C Self-Check.

☐ Did you write any sentence fragments? If so, correct them.

☐ Do you have a clear topic sentence?

☐ Is your writing interesting? Could you add any more details?

Your Free Time

PREVIEW

1 **Answer the questions.**

1. How does the Internet help people save time? ....
....

2. List some ways the Internet takes away from people's free time. ....
....
....

3. Do you consider surfing the Web a leisure activity? Why or why not? ....
....
....

2 **What About You? Complete the survey.**

> **About how much time do you spend on the Internet each day?** ....
>
> **What do you do on the Internet? Check all the activities you engage in.**
>
> ○ e-mail   ○ music
>
> ○ news   ○ chat/instant messaging
>
> ○ games   ○ information searches
>
> ○ shopping   ○ surfing
>
> ○ banking   ○ other: ....
>
> **Do you think you spend too much time online?** ....
>
> **If you didn't have Internet access, what would you spend more time doing?**
>
> ....
> ....

Factoid   South Koreans spend more time surfing the Web than any other nation, at an average of 16 hours and 17 minutes spent each month.

SOURCES: www.bizjournals.com, www.acnielsen.com

3 Challenge. Look at the graphs. What happens as people spend more time on the Internet? Write sentences about each graph, using double comparatives. Refer to Student's Book page 88 if you need to review double comparatives.

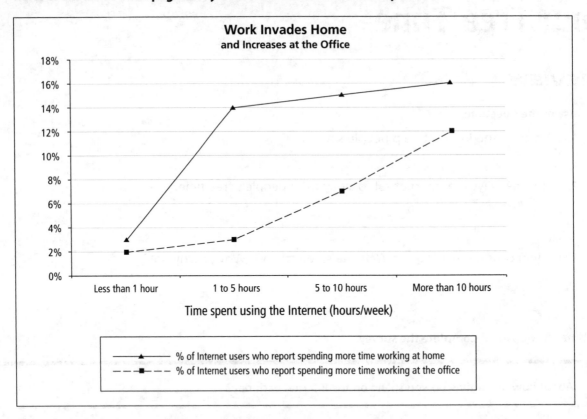

1. *The more time people spend on the Internet, the more time they spend working at home.*

2. _____

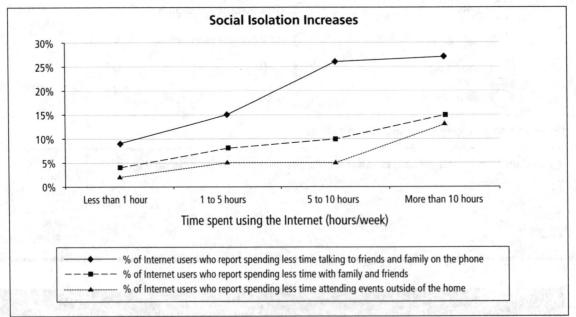

SOURCE: Time Study Project, Stanford Institute for the Quantitative Study of Society (SIQSS)

3. _____

4. _____

5. _____

LESSON 1

4 Give your opinion of the leisure activities below. Use adjectives from the box or your own adjectives.

annoying	challenging	difficult	entertaining	fascinating	interesting	stimulating
boring	costly	dull	exciting	fun	relaxing	unusual

1. Go: *I've never played, but I think Go sounds fascinating.*

2. Karate: ....

3. Chess: ....

4. Aerobics: ....

5. Yoga: ....

6. Ping-pong: ....

7. Embroidery: ....

8. Wood carving: ....

5 Think of an activity that you are interested in taking up and one that you are <u>not</u> interested in. Use them to complete the two conversations below.

A: You should give .... a try. I'm sure you'd like it.

You: ....

A: You should give .... a try. I'm sure you'd like it.

You: ....

6 Complete each collocation for leisure activities with the correct verb. Then, circle the adverbs and underline the words or phrases they modify. Finally, write <u>V</u> (verb) or <u>A</u> (adjective) above each underlined word or phrase.

1. I .... yoga. It's a great workout, and I find it emotionally soothing.

2. I .... video games. I know what you're thinking, but video games do have benefits. My favorite ones are intellectually stimulating.

3. My friends and I .... embroidery. Not only is it a fun way to interact socially, but it also pays off financially. We sell what we make.

4. I .... antiques – mostly furniture. It keeps me busy and active. It's actually a lot more physically demanding than most people realize.

What leisure activity do you do? What are the benefits? Use an adverb in your answer.

....

....

LESSON 2

7 Describe the clothing, shoes, and accessories you're wearing right now. Use as many modifiers as you can.

Example: *I'm wearing my comfortable new green leather boots.*

_____

_____

8 In the circles below are collectors' names and the objects they collect. Surrounding each circle are modifiers describing the most valuable item in each collection. Write a one-sentence description of each item, using the words from the diagram.

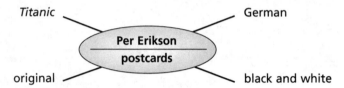

Titanic · · · German

Per Erikson
postcards

original · · · black and white

1. *Per Erikson has an original black-and-white German Titanic postcard.*

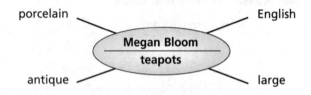

porcelain · · · English

Megan Bloom
teapots

antique · · · large

2. _____

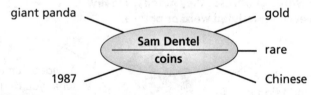

giant panda · · · gold

Sam Dentel
coins

· rare

1987 · · · Chinese

3. **(Challenge)** _____

Now think of something special that you have. Write the item and words to describe it in the diagram.

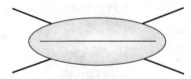

Use the modifiers from your diagram to write a one-sentence description of your item.

_____

9 Complete the second sentence in each pair, using a compound modifier. Remember to hyphenate.

1. This vase is three hundred years old. It's a .... vase.

2. Yoga classes usually last one and a half hours. They're .... classes.

3. The diamond in her ring is two carats. She has a .... diamond ring.

4. The book I'm reading has nine hundred pages. It's a .... book.

5. The Internet was invented in the twentieth century. It's a .... invention.

6. That mountain bike costs a thousand dollars. It's a .... mountain bike.

LESSON 3

10 How do new technological tools make people's lives easier? How do they take away from leisure time? Name one positive aspect and one negative aspect of each of the technologies listed.

Technology	Positive	Negative
cell phones		
PDAs		
laptops		
e-mail		
voice mail		

11 Read the article on Student's Book page 116 again. Then complete the sentence below in three different ways, using double comparatives.

According to the author, the more we use new technological tools, . . .

. . . .

. . . .

. . . .

12 Think about your day yesterday. Answer the questions.

1. How many hours did you spend working or studying? ....

2. How much free time did you have? What did you do? ....

3. If you work, did you work after hours? What technological tools did you use to do your work?
....

4. Did you talk to any friends yesterday? If so, did you see them in person, talk to them on the phone, or send them an e-mail or an instant message? ....
....

13 Look at the list of technological tools below. First, circle the ones you have or use. Then, indicate how difficult it would be for you to live without each.

How difficult would it be to live without _____?	not difficult at all	somewhat difficult	extremely difficult
a cell phone	○	○	○
a PDA	○	○	○
a laptop	○	○	○
e-mail	○	○	○
the Internet	○	○	○
voice mail	○	○	○
a fax machine	○	○	○

According to a survey done by the British magazine *Personnel Today* and Websense International, 72% of British companies have dealt with employees' accessing the Internet for personal use.

SOURCE: www.out-law.com

Of the technological tools listed, which would be the most difficult for you to live without? Why?

....

....

14 Reading. Read the article.

Work at Home, Play at Work

Thanks to the Internet and other relatively new technological tools, more and more employees work after hours. They check their e-mail before they go to bed at night, take business calls while out to dinner with friends, and check their PDAs at family picnics. Nowadays, if you're sick, you don't have to take a day off. Why waste a day sleeping and watching movies when, with a laptop and an Internet connection, you can work from home? It seems that the line between work and leisure has become blurry and that more technology for work has meant less time for ourselves.

However, technology has not only helped work invade people's leisure time, but it has also allowed people to engage in leisure-time activities at work. With the computer on your office desk, you can leave work virtually. You can check the score of last night's game, do a little shopping, catch up on the news, order concert tickets, plan a vacation, chat with your friends, or just browse the Web. You can appear to be working hard—plugging away at your computer—when in reality you're reading a fashion magazine online.

According to a recent survey by California-based Websense, more than half of the employees questioned said they spent between one and five hours a day surfing the Internet at work for personal reasons. There are even websites dedicated to keeping bored workers amused while they wait for the end of the work day. A psychotherapist who treats Internet addiction explains, "It's like having a TV at everyone's desk. People can watch whatever they want and do whatever they want."

Perhaps a more definite separation of work and home life would be better not only for employees but also for employers. It's not healthy for workers to have access to work 24/7*. And maybe if employees weren't busy working at night and on the weekends, they wouldn't have to e-mail their friends while they're at work.

* 24/7 = 24 hours a day, 7 days a week

SOURCE: www.post-gazette.com

Now complete each sentence with a word or phrase from the article.

1. If something is not clear, it's ....

2. When something unwanted interferes with your time, it .... your time.

3. If you do something on a computer, rather than in the real world, you do it ....

4. If you're working hard at something, you're .... at it.

5. If you do something all the time, you do it ....

15 **Answer the questions, using information from the article in Exercise 14.**

1. What are some ways people are able to work from home? ....

....

2. What are some ways people are able to engage in leisure-time activities at work?

....

3. What's the author's point of view in the article? ....

....

4. Do you agree with the author's point of view? Why or why not? ....

....

LESSON 4

16 **What's your opinion? Place each of the extreme sports under one of the four categories in the chart.**

bungee jumping	mountain biking	surfing
extreme skiing	rock climbing	waterfall jumping
hang gliding	skydiving	white water rafting

I've already done it.	I can't wait to try it.	It could be fun.	Not a chance!

17 Take the quiz to see if you have a risk-taking personality.

---

www.adventurequiz.com

QUIZ Are you a risk taker or a risk avoider?

1. Which type of movie would you rather watch?
   - ⊙ **a.** scary
   - ⊙ **b.** funny

2. Which would you rather do at an amusement park?
   - ⊙ **a.** go on a roller coaster
   - ⊙ **b.** see a show

3. Which sentence describes you better?
   - ⊙ **a.** I love trying new things.
   - ⊙ **b.** I prefer to stick close to home.

4. Which genre of music would you rather listen to?
   - ⊙ **a.** urban dance
   - ⊙ **b.** pop

5. What kind of clothes do you wear? Pick one adjective from each pair.
   - ⊙ **a.** trendy
   - ⊙ **b.** classic
   - ⊙ **a.** flashy
   - ⊙ **b.** subdued
   - ⊙ **a.** shocking
   - ⊙ **b.** tasteful

6. Which do you prefer? Pick one choice from each pair.
   - ⊙ **a.** to stand out in a crowd
   - ⊙ **b.** to conform
   - ⊙ **a.** fast-paced city life
   - ⊙ **b.** slower pace of the country or suburbs

7. What are your shopping habits?
   - ⊙ **a.** impulse buying
   - ⊙ **b.** comparison shopping

8. How do you spend your free time?
   - ⊙ **a.** I find something exciting to do.
   - ⊙ **b.** I catch up on work and chores.

9. Which would you rather take up?
   - ⊙ **a.** karate
   - ⊙ **b.** embroidery

10. Pick the adjective or phrase that best describes you from each of the following pairs.
    - ⊙ **a.** thrill-seeking
    - ⊙ **b.** conservative
    - ⊙ **a.** rebellious
    - ⊙ **b.** obedient
    - ⊙ **a.** aggressive
    - ⊙ **b.** cautious
    - ⊙ **a.** adventurous
    - ⊙ **b.** prefer routine
    - ⊙ **a.** a troublemaker
    - ⊙ **b.** well-behaved
    - ⊙ **a.** self-confident
    - ⊙ **b.** nervous
    - ⊙ **a.** energetic
    - ⊙ **b.** calm
    - ⊙ **a.** outgoing
    - ⊙ **b.** shy

Count up your score.
How many <u>a</u>'s did you check? _____
How many <u>b</u>'s did you check? _____

0–5 <u>a</u> answers: You probably have a "small T" personality. You don't like thrills and prefer to avoid them. You're among the faint of heart. You prefer certainty and routine. But don't get too set in your ways. A little adventure from time to time would do you some good.

6–11 <u>a</u> answers: You fall somewhere in the middle of the risk-taking continuum. You're probably willing to take some risks from time to time, but maybe prefer to avoid risk in general. Sounds like you live a pretty balanced life.

12–20 <u>a</u> answers: You probably have a "big T" personality. You love thrills and can't get enough of them. You're happiest living on the edge. You like to take risks and do new things. Remember: risk-taking can be the key to success, but it can also get you into trouble. Make an effort to exercise some caution.

How do your quiz results compare with your answer to Exercise B on Student's Book page 118? If they differ, which do you think is more accurate? Explain.

....

....

 . . . it is uninteresting to do easy things. We find out about ourselves only when we take risks, when we challenge and question.
—Magdalena Abakanowicz, Polish artist, born 1930

Source: www.wisdomquotes.com

Grammar Booster

A **Complete the sentences with appropriate intensifiers.**

1. He has a .... interesting hobby.

2. I find yoga .... boring.

3. My mother is .... interested in ancient history.

4. She's .... good about keeping in touch with her friends.

5. He's a .... skilled dancer.

6. Our company uses some .... advanced technology.

7. Mr. James is .... busy at work right now.

8. She says that playing the guitar is .... challenging.

B **Complete the sentences with adverbs of manner from the box. Use each adverb only once.**

angrily	beautifully	fairly	hard	softly	quickly

1. We walked ...., because we were late.

2. Their daughter was sleeping, so they spoke ....

3. After arguing with his father, he .... left the room.

4. She's quite a musician. She plays the clarinet ....

5. You must treat your friends ....

6. Mrs. Young works .... all week long.

C **Write your own sentences, using the adverbs in parentheses.**

1. (well) ....

2. (poorly) ....

3. (suddenly) ....

4. (sadly) ....

5. (slowly) ....

Writing: *Comment on another's point of view*

A **Prewriting. Developing arguments.**

Read the article "Work at Home, Play at Work" on page 96 and underline sentences that you agree with or do not agree with. Then do the following:

- Paraphrase each sentence you underlined.

- Provide the reasons why you agree or disagree.

> *The author says that technology has allowed people to engage in leisure-time activities at work. I agree because I know a lot of people who use the Internet at work for personal reasons.*

....
....
....
....
....
....
....

B **Writing.** Write a critique of the article. State your own opinion at the beginning. Use the sentences you underlined and the comments you wrote to support your opinion.

....
....
....
....
....
....
....
....
....
....
....
....
....

C **Self-Check.**

☐ Is your opinion clearly stated?

☐ Did you use connecting words to support your reasons and sequence your ideas?

☐ Did you use quotation marks when using the author's own words?

☐ Did you paraphrase the author's words when you didn't use direct speech?